MAXIMS AND REFLECTIONS

WINSTON S. CHURCHILL'S

Maxims
and
Reflections

Selected by COLIN COOTE and

DENZIL BATCHELOR; with an

Introduction by COLIN COOTE

BARNES
&NOBLE
BOOKS
NEW YORK

This edition published by Barnes & Noble Inc.

1992 Barnes & Noble Books

ISBN 0-88029-813-8

Printed and bound in the United States of America

M 9 8 7 6 5 4 3 2 1

N T S

PREFACE

THE source and, in most cases, the date of the quotations of which this book is composed have been included, because it is important not only to know what was said, but when it was said, and how. The elucidatory notes subjoined to many are the minimum necessary to point the moral and to adorn or understand the tale.

I do not know whether any corns will be sensitised by the inclusion of references to Southern Ireland in the chapter on Foreigners. Probably not; for I remember that when I was a correspondent in Rome the Southern Irish used to be exasperated by the Italian persistence in calling them 'English Catholics'.

The classification of quotations has been difficult. It is always easier to divide a person's life into stages than his sayings into subjects. Readers may therefore sometimes think that a quotation has been misplaced, but there has always been a reason either of time or of context for putting it where it is.

I am indebted to Messrs. George G. Harrap & Co. Ltd. for permission to quote from *Marlborough* and from *Arms and the Covenant*, and to Messrs. Odhams Press for similar permission in respect of the other works of Mr. Churchill. I am also most grateful to Mr. Churchill himself for approving and endorsing the project of the present anthology.

February 1947.   C. R. C.

INTRODUCTION

THE first time I remember hearing of Mr. Churchill was when my father—no mean politician himself—told my mother at breakfast that 'Randolph's son' seemed to have waked up the House of Commons the night before. I fancy that must have been the speech in which he criticised the conduct of the South African War. The first time I remember hearing Mr. Churchill—and therefore indubitably the first time I heard him, for one does not forget hearing him—was at a meeting of prospective Coalition Liberal candidates before the election of 1918. A slightly bent figure with a slightly echoing articulation gave us a few words of greeting and exhortation. I do not recall what they were, but I recall very well the personality who uttered them. It was like strychnine. You were not very sure whether it was a tonic or a poison, but you were very sure it was very powerful.

That seems to be not uncommonly the impact of Mr. Churchill's personality upon his fellows, and the excitation of extremes of feeling is one of the hall-marks of great men. Their friends and their enemies are equally obsessed; and it may well be that the verdict of history upon them depends upon the mere accident whether the words or writings which survive are those of a friend or of an enemy. Though it might be disastrous to spread the speculation among schoolboys, it is permissible to ask whether the great historians of antiquity were great judges or great liars. In any case, impartial writers are of a sickening prolixity and dullness. It is better, on all counts, to apply a broad brush, whether it be charged with whitewash or with tar. Look back on the whole mass of a man's life. Does it exhale an odour of sweetness or of corruption? If the former, why spend time in sniffing for a taint? If the latter, why spend time in searching for roses among the carrion? 'We are all of us in the gutter, but some of us are looking at the stars.' The best course, therefore, is to give humble thanks when an astronomer is found among the guttersnipes.

Let me therefore try to avoid both picking holes to the extent of failing to reveal the pattern of the cloth and pretending that my cloth has no holes. The first task will be easier than the second; for it is surely the bounden duty of any writer to admit that he owes to Mr. Churchill more than to any other living Englishman the fact that he can still write what he likes.

The purpose of this volume is to show in Mr. Churchill's own words what he is like as a man, a statesman, an orator, and a writer. Let me take the last manifestation first, and claim that posterity will be grateful that there is no 'closed shop' in journalism or authorship. Mr. Churchill owes much to Gibbon, but there is something in his writing all his own. Somebody once said that Gibbon gave the reader an impression of reclining sagely and majestically on Olympus and watching pigmies rushing or manœuvring about below—or words to that effect. Mr. Churchill carries one down to the pigmies and makes them human beings, but provides one with a return ticket to Olympus. Compare Gibbon's famous epigram on the younger Gordian, 'Twenty-two acknowledged concubines and a library of sixty-two thousand volumes attested the variety of his inclinations', with Mr. Churchill's verdict on the Margrave of Baden, 'His military epitaph for all time must be that the two greatest captains of the age rated, by actions more expressive than words, his absence from a battlefield well worth 15,000 men.' The former tickles the reader into a slightly salacious smile—it is the club wit at his best after a bottle of the club's best port. The latter is the kind of wit sometimes, but all too rarely, heard in the House of Commons, clean and devastating, inducing first a gasp and then a roar.

That is not to say that Mr. Churchill is always original. Nobody soaked in history ever is, because, consciously or unconsciously, in any situation they remember that it has happened before and what were the reactions on noble spirits. Thus in the dark hours of May 1940 Mr. Churchill's stern and stimulating promise of 'blood, toil, tears, and sweat' was a direct echo of Garibaldi's address to his followers after the defence of the Roman Republic had collapsed and he was about to start on his march across Italy. Or again, when, in his first speech as Prime Minister, Mr. Churchill defined his policy as 'to make war', he was echoing Clemenceau's 'Je fais la guerre'; and the famous passage in a later speech about fighting 'on the beaches, in the hills, in the streets' recalls the same leader's fierce declamation in 1918: 'I shall fight in front of Paris, within Paris, behind Paris.'

But, as I say, there is a tang of his own about Mr. Churchill. Indeed, his writing is like his oratory. It is essentially cut and thrust. He is the champion

whether in attack or defence of some cause or person.
Whether the word is written or spoken, the technique
is the same. The available evidence is soberly mar-
shalled, with sufficient embellishment of phrase to
sustain the interest of the uninstructed and sufficient
profundity of information to sustain the interest of the
expert. Then there is a pause, more evident, of course,
in speech than in writing, though the reader can sense
the pen quivering just as the audience can see the eye
twinkling. Finally, out it comes—a phrase or a word
summarising what he has had in mind all through the
preparatory period. One example from his writings
must suffice. He has been giving an account of the
Battle of Jutland which certainly lacks nothing in technical detail. He describes at each of the three main
crises of the operation the courses open to the British
Commander-in-Chief, and how upon each, by some
fatality, not the most fruitful was followed; and he
ends simply by saying: 'Three times is a lot.' From
the speeches, an example as good as any is the famous
tailpiece to the account of the Battle of Britain: 'Never
in the history of human conflict was so much owed by
so many to so few.' I also recall one supremely brilliant phrase, when he congratulated Mr. Baldwin with
just the right touch of envy on having among 'the most
important arts of his armoury the successful avowal of
mistakes'.

No doubt the similarities between the speeches and
the writings are because Mr. Churchill usually dictates
his books and writes his orations. (Personally, I don't
think it matters much how one achieves the written
word, provided that one does nct use a typewriter. I

think that instrument is fatal to the writing of good English. How can thought flow smoothly when it has to be transferred to that clacking, clinking, checking monstrosity?) He has himself described the pains of preparation which result in what so often sounds spontaneous; and how his maiden speech had to be launched by a kindly piece of prompting from Mr. Gibson Bowles. But in fact he has for long been a master of impromptu. What could be better than the retort to the M.P. who was bouncing up and down in a series of angry interruptions—'The honourable Gentleman should really not generate more indignation than he can conveniently contain'?

There is, moreover, one form of speaking in which Mr. Churchill excels, though it is impossible to illustrate his eloquence by citation. This is conversation —talk on those private occasions when language is given us to reveal and not to conceal our thoughts. The conditions requisite for conversation are that bodies should be relaxed but minds active; that the company should be congenial though of varied opinions; that nobody should be in a hurry; and that there should be a certain moderate lubrication of the inner man. It is easy to see how the complexity of modern existence and, more recently, the impact of rationing have destroyed the opportunities for this fertile and fruitful form of human intercourse. But it survives in odd corners, and those fortunate enough to find Mr. Churchill in one of them will have a pleasant evening. 'Churchill,' the late President Roosevelt is reported to have said, 'has a hundred ideas a day, of which at least four are good ideas.' Well, four are a lot.

It is therefore quite untrue that the figure which he cuts as a master of language owes everything to the corsets of preparation. He has a natural taste for the delicacies of the English tongue, which is, indeed, the supreme instrument both for delicacy and indelicacy. A case can be made out that it is the best language in which to write lyric poetry and the best language in which to swear. For myself, I think that however good the instrument and the technical use of it, the effect of oratory depends very largely on the orator's voice. Not only what the orator says, but how he says it is important. It is even true to-day that the most effective speaker over the wireless is not the most effective to an audience. Lord Baldwin, for example, was much better over the air than on the ground, so to say; and if we were to revive the classical schools of rhetoric, they might do worse than study why some disembodied voices are so much better than others. It is so. As for Mr. Churchill, he is pretty good at both, but, in my opinion, not quite so good over the wireless. It is not the gestures that one misses, for he uses few gestures. I think the inability to see the facial expressions as he works through and up to his points is one reason. Another may be that an audience is necessary for some speakers to give of their best—the corporative mind reacts on the individual mind, and vice versa. Soliloquy does not suit Mr. Churchill. He is, first and foremost, a House of Commons man. Parliament is his natural platform, or grindstone, or touchstone. Incidentally, there is no audience which can better silence the bore or spur the brilliant.

The calibre of an orator must be assessed relatively

as well as absolutely. It has been my fate to hear (and to understand) orators of many nations; and I have an admiration for anybody who can make a speech, because I am wholly incapable of making one myself. I can say, therefore, with complete objectivity, that Mussolini could be a finer actor, Briand more persuasive, Viviani more polished, Lloyd George more witty, Lord Birkenhead more trenchant. But none of these gave the same impression of power and sincerity as Mr. Churchill. (Incidentally, I could never understand Hitler's undoubted successes with his audiences. Goebbels was far better.) On great occasions, he does not seem to have to find the *mot juste*—it seems to be given to him. The quality of oratory consists not merely in arousing emotions, but also, if need be, in calming them. Personally, therefore, I am not inclined to rank even his finest war speeches as necessarily his best. Any man with any gift of speech at all would have caught inspiration from the grimly ecstatic courage of those times. The best speech, *qua* speech, is surely that which makes head against a current. On this view the two speeches which I would select as Mr. Churchill's best are that which he made in the debate on the Amritsar shooting and that which he made on the Munich agreement. In the first, he faced a House vehemently hostile, bored it into calmness with a disquisition on military law, and then caught its interest with exactly the same arguments as those which, in another's mouth, had roused it to fury. In the second, he had to make head against the almost hysterical relief that war had been averted. He gained no new converts, but he made the hysterical 'think it possible that they were mistaken'.

There is one other speech of Mr. Churchill's which, in racing parlance, is worthy of a place. It was made in the debate on the murder of Sir Henry Wilson by an Irish gunman—a debate which found the Home Secretary of the day unable to make head against charges of inadequate security precautions. The Colonial Secretary, as Mr. Churchill then was, came to the rescue and saved the Parliamentary day. It is to be observed that two out of the three speeches selected changed, and the third shook, the prevalent opinion of the House of Commons. To have done either of these things is an achievement of which any statesman can be proud. In an experience of Parliament extending over nearly thirty years I can count the occasions on which it has been done on the fingers of two hands. Where Mr. Churchill is exceptional is that there is always a chance of his doing it. To those who may think that the terrible difficulty of the task is a reflection on the capacity of M.P.s, I must point out that, if it were easy, stability of Government would become impossible; and it is precisely in its quality of stability that the British Parliamentary system is superior to others of the same stamp. The Americans, of course, also have stability; but in their case it is procured by a written and rigid constitution, which too often changes the stable into the sourly stagnant.

One further comment is necessary before leaving the assessment of Mr. Churchill as a writer and orator. His prose, whether written or spoken, has a rhythm and cadence, which do not, indeed, conform to any rules of scansion, but are consistently notable. You get the same kind of arrangement of words, so that they flow instead of staggering, in the orations of Cicero; and I think this is instinctive rather than deliberate. Any competent journalist knows that a passage, though grammatically correct, may look clumsy. The knack is acquired—it may even be a natural gift—of writing with balance or, if you prefer the term, musically. That does not mean writing or speaking pontifically or using long and recondite words. Mr. Churchill's writings and speeches are, as already noted, Gibbonian—that is to say, they are mouth- and brain-filling. But they are wholly different from the horrible jargon in which so many of our State papers and Acts of Parliament are couched. Mr. Churchill's tilt against this depart-mentalese during the war was certainly one of the four good ideas which he had on the day when he delivered it; but the wound, if any, which his lance inflicted has unhappily not proved mortal. We still have to endure such distortions as saying 'of the order of' when what is meant is 'about' or 'approximately'. The relapse does not detract from the merit of Mr. Churchill's effort to save both English and England.

A man who has held almost every high office under the Crown has a great presumptive claim to be reckoned as statesman. But there have been many who have held high offices without adorning all or any of them. The number of Mr. Churchill's posts do not, therefore, in themselves create a pedestal. Let us see if there is more solid material.

In the first place, Mr. Churchill certainly deserves better than to be known for his foibles. For example, the British public were long more intrigued by the queerness of his hats than by what was underneath

them. Again, everybody knows that he likes laying
bricks, but that does not mean that he is liable to drop
them. He is also known to be a better painter than
Hitler, but that does not mean that he is a worse politician. He is known to like cigars, but that does not
mean that he emits nothing except smoke. He is said
to like old brandy, but he is certainly not 'wet' in
the more derogatory meaning of the word. This is
not the place to discuss the drink question; but it must
be observed that one survival from the age of rotten
boroughs is the rotten insinuation that men in the public eye are alcoholics. It is the favourite scandal, from
which few, except those whose appearance and pro-
fessions belie it, are immune. The best comment on it
is that made by the French wit, who wrote under an
advertisement which said, 'L'Alcohol tue lentement'

'Tant mieux. Nous ne sommes pas pressés.'

In the second place, Mr. Churchill is not to be judged
by some of the impressions commonly held or manu-
factured about his career. In particular, the charge of
political inconsistency is utterly misleading. He started
as a Tory, became a Liberal, then a Coalition Liberal,
then a Constitutionalist, and finally a Tory again. But
the variations were not due to variations in his beliefs.
He was not 'genuinely seeking work', as was so cruelly
said of another statesman who changed his party. The
kind of Toryism with which he started was the Tory
Democracy of his father, that gifted and tragic figure
who captured his son's so fervent admiration by such
slender and almost casual contacts. The true home of

the Tory Democrat of the early years of this century was not the Tory party as it then was. His proper place was in the Liberal party, which resembled Heaven at least in having many mansions, one of which housed the Liberal Imperialists. From under that roof he could combine a passionate advocacy of social reform (part of which in those days was the defence of Free Trade—the object of the official Tory party's attack) with a zealous concern for the British Empire.

One of the regrettable consequences of the first World War was the disintegration of the Liberal party. The Radical tail, under the new and masterly name of the Labour party, wagged most of the dog; and the adoption of the animal's individualistic bark by the Conservative party was a natural consequence of a new dividing-line in British politics between Socialists and Capitalists. There could be no question about which side of the line Mr. Churchill would find the more congenial. He has been responsible for many measures of social reform; he has even favoured for purely practical reasons proposals essentially Socialistic, such as the nationalisation of the railways. But the idea of the Socialist State is repugnant to him.

The migration back to the Tory party coincided with a new impulse in that party towards social reform, and was as natural to Mr. Churchill as the exodus from it in 1902. He has, in fact, always been essentially a Coalitionist. The causes in which he profoundly believes transcend the strict limits of the doctrines of any one party; and he is not at his happiest as the party man—not even, perhaps, as the party chief.

For that reason he is not even a very good electioneerer. From the error of tactics in his first by-election, which caused the late Lord Balfour to say 'I thought he was a young man of promise. It appears he is only a young man of promises', to the remarkable incident in 1945 when an unknown incoherent polled ten thousand votes against the Prime Minister who had won the war, his seats have never long been really comfortable. Dundee, for example, which serenely voted him in from 1908 to 1918, voted him out in 1922 with a savagery which, at the time, greatly impressed and perplexed him.

The truth is that the electorate has, among other resemblances to Providence, a habit of moving 'in mysterious ways its wonders to perform'. It is sometimes excruciatingly faithful to duds and fickle to celebrities. In Mr. Churchill's case, the fact is that he has never possessed a territorial base like Mr. Lloyd George in Wales or the Chamberlains in Birmingham. Britain is his constituency and not any particular part of it, nor any particular party in it. There is the clearest evidence that at any great crisis in our affairs his natural instinct is to search for a national Government. He has a conviction that patriotism *is* enough, and labels do not very much matter.

So much for the famous 'inconsistency'. In fact, it is doubtful whether the quality of a statesman is to be judged by any such test as fidelity to a party. If Charles James Fox had remained all his life of the party of the 'King's Friends', he could not have been reckoned a statesman at all. The true test is surely the power to inspire, to create, to foresee, to understand, and to be inspired; and these qualities must be possessed not only in conception, but in execution. The finest idea is useless if it is incompetently carried out.

Nobody has ever accused Mr. Churchill of being short of ideas. His judgment has indeed been questioned—by Mr. Neville Chamberlain; and the reason for these questionings may be found in his own remark: 'I have a tendency, against which I should, perhaps, be on my guard, to swim against the stream.' Sometimes, of course, the stream is right—as it was on the question of the abdication, or (at least, so it seems to me) on the question of Indian self-government. But sometimes also the swimmer against it has been right. For example, he was a thousand times right in urging the forcing of the Dardanelles in 1915; and I fancy there is nothing in his whole career, not even the defeat of his Government in the General Election of 1945, which has left behind it such a taste and tang of bitterness as the frustration by fate and fools of the Gallipoli expedition. Again, he was all too right about the menace of Hitler, though in that case the current against him was not a stream, but a tide; and, like a tide, it turned. I shall always think that this period in his career was in many respects his 'finest hour'. Nobody who has not had the experience can imagine how unpleasant it is to face a hostile House of Commons, savagely resolved to shout or sneer one into silence.

'Forgiveness to the injured doth belong,
But he ne'er pardons who has done the wrong.'

When the House is determined to be wrong it cannot forgive anybody who persists in proving that it is wrong. The hostile atmosphere of Westminster spreads through the Press and the public, like the smell of cooking through a boarding-house. The only doubtful question about the object of this hostility is whether he is more knave or fool; and it becomes as hard for him to stage a comeback as for a discredited pugilist. For some six years Mr. Churchill was exposed to this all-pervasive hostility. He never winced nor wilted. That alone would establish his claim to be a statesman.

But, after all, it is the man behind all these manifestations of the man who is the most interesting. About the man—and about the boy, too—there is one outstanding characteristic, namely, a zest for living which has become all too rare in these harassed times. 'Twenty to twenty-five! Those are the years!' says Mr. Churchill himself. But nobody has less reason to sigh over the days that have fled; for the vital spark that coruscates so splendidly in youth has, in his case, continued to sparkle past the allotted span.

It seems hard to recapture in days when danger is faced no less firmly but far more as a duty the spirit which was drawn to face danger for its own sake, as steel is drawn to a magnet. I would not disparage the modern generation. Indeed, theirs may well be the truer courage, since they face unflinchingly perils about which, at first hand or vicariously, they know all, so that the glamour has departed and only the hard skeleton of horror remains. Nevertheless, the 'panache' of the pre-1914 generation of young men was attractive; and those who regret its passing may find the gist of it in Mr. Churchill. The reader may take

exception to the choice of a French term to describe
the chief characteristic of an Englishman. But it is
not inappropriate to Mr. Churchill, whose French
vocabulary is more extensive and whose French accent
is more execrable than that of most of our nation. He
has also always had a certain inclination towards
the French. Is it not recorded that Clemenceau
said of him, 'M. Churchill est loin d'être un
ennemi de la France', a verdict which, in the Tiger,
was purring indeed? It is not, however, true that Mr.
Churchill's feelings for the French were undiscrimina-
ting. There is a tale of a retort to General de Gaulle
. . . But that, as Mr. Kipling used to say, is another
story. He is, nevertheless, in tune with French civilisation. He likes its long and spirited tradition, its determined individualism, the 'furia franchese' which applies
not only to French troops, but is an intensity of spirit
which enables its possessors to be sometimes only a
little lower than the angels—though also sometimes
only a little higher than the devils. There is certainly
no other foreigner who could have shown such a brilliant and generous understanding as Mr. Churchill
showed in his broadcast to the French people after the
capitulation. From the first phrase, 'I repeat the
legend around the louis d'or, "Dieu protége la
France" ', to the last 'Sleep now' it was exactly
right.

A psychiatrist might possibly trace Mr. Churchill's
interest in the French back to the fact that they were
the adversaries over whom his ancestor the great Duke
of Marlborough triumphed, and were thus the cause
of his glory. But the explanation is simpler than that.

It may be, as he modestly says himself, that he drifted or stumbled into the Army originally because his father happened to see him and his brother Jack marshalling armies of toy soldiers. Nevertheless, a passionate interest in the reading, writing, and, it may be added, making of military history has always possessed him; and you can't study the subject without everywhere tripping over the French.

Indeed, probably any nation which puts up a good show gains his respect. The first strong stroke which he made against any stream was his appreciative remark about the Boers in arms against us. He does not like the Germans; but even in their case his book on the 1914-18 war ends with a magnificent catalogue of their efforts and the phrase: 'Surely, Germans, for history it is enough.'

Be that as it may, Mr. Churchill has undoubtedly a military temperament. That does not in the least mean that he is, as he has frequently been accused of being, a 'warmonger'. On the contrary, the true soldier has, even more than the civilian, a horror of war; and it is a fact that whenever Mr. Churchill is called upon to drink a loyal toast he invariably adds to 'The King' the *sotto voce* prayer 'and no war'. The military mind, in his sense, is one interested indeed in the technical conduct of war, but no less in the problem of how war can be avoided. There comes a point, which such a mind recognises and fears before it arises to the view of all men, when life must be risked to save all that makes life worth living; and there is nothing bellicose about fighting then with all one's might and main up to and beyond the edge of endurance. Mr. Churchill has nothing in common with pacifists, but he has nothing in common with Jingoes either.

How does he rank as a soldier? I do not mean as the pert and pushing subaltern, who pulled strings to get into action and used pens to describe it—both in a shockingly successful way. I mean as a strategist whether at the Admiralty in the first World War or as Minister of Defence and Prime Minister in the second. As for 1914-18, something has already been said about the Dardanelles; and Mr. Churchill's share in the development of the tank may be added to his claims to fame during that period. They were indeed endorsed by the simple fact that when, in 1939, he returned to the Admiralty on the outbreak of war an exhilarated whisper ran round the Navy: 'Winnie is back.'

During the last war the test was, of course, much sterner. It will, I think, be admitted that the main strategic decisions all through were Mr. Churchill's. At least (to echo Marshal Joffre's reply to the question who won the Battle of the Marne), the blame if these decisions had been wrong would have been laid upon him; and there were occasionally whimsical or malicious whispers that he fancied himself to be the reincarnation of Marlborough. Moreover, war, in our country and under our Constitution, is run by a committee composed wholly or mainly of civilians over which the Prime Minister presides; and the decisions of committees over which Mr. Churchill presides are liable to be Mr. Churchill's. He was not, like Hitler, surrounded by mere toadies, and it is not suggested that Cabinet meetings were occasions for burning incense before 'the greatest strategic genius of all time'. I only mean that, though the team was good, he was the undisputed captain of it.

But there is another feature of our constitutional practice, which has developed through sub-committees of the Committee of Imperial Defence, namely, that the committee of civilians never acts without the advice of military experts. That does not diminish their responsibility; and when the experts disagree, as they sometimes do, the civilians have to decide. I mention the experts particularly because Mr. Churchill was always extremely sensitive to their advice—perhaps this sensitiveness was a reaction from the Dardanelles experience. He worked them hard. He worked them at queer hours, because of his practice of taking a nap in the afternoons and of being particularly active through a large part of the night. But he listened to them. Unlike Hitler, he was not guided purely by his intuition.

Such is the background to the great strategic decisions of the war. Let us list some of them. I do not include the decision to fight on alone after the fall of France, because if ever there was a decision of a whole nation and not of any man or group in it, that was the one. Indeed, Mr. Churchill himself has said of the first Cabinet meeting over which he presided that if anybody had even hinted at anything like giving in that person would have been torn to pieces. But no similar pre-judgment governed the decision to send our first, and at that time our only armoured, division to Africa in the autumn of 1940 instead of keeping it at home; nor the refusal to open a Second Front in Europe until it could be more than a forlorn hope; nor the steady devotion of so much of our resources (though not as much as Air Marshal Harris wanted) to building up the bomber offensive. These were crucial decisions; and they were sound, marked alike by daring and by discernment.

Mr. Churchill is more than a descendant of the Duke of Marlborough. He is also half American; and it is perhaps from across the Atlantic that a touch of restlessness and even of flamboyance in him originates. But personally I consider all talk of national characteristics to be more or less rubbish; and if asked to place Mr. Churchill in any special category, I should prefer the criterion to be a period rather than a country. In many ways he belongs to the second half of the eighteenth century, when, at least for a considerable part of society, life was brilliant and assured and ideas fresh and blazing. There should be nothing offensive in talking about a 'governing class' in a country where entry into it is open to people of all classes. Some are qualified, others qualify for it; and it is stupid to say that only those who qualify for it without originally belonging to it should govern. Well, Mr. Churchill does belong to it. He would have qualified if he had not belonged, but belong to it he does, not because of his birth or even his cigars, but because of his temperament. He was certainly born in the political purple, but he wears it as to the manner born, and not all sons of famous fathers can say that.

That temperament has, admittedly, the defects of its qualities. A man who knows what he wants and thinks it natural that he should get it is not a good listener. It

is not only fools that he does not suffer gladly. Or—
to put the same point in another way—when ideas
and arguments boil and bubble up ceaselessly in a
human brain its possessor is liable to sweep aside any
interruption. You can turn off a tap, but not a spring.

It is not that he resents interruption or opposition
—he just disregards them. Yet there are exceptions
to this indifference. I have heard it said that Mr.
Churchill has had few intimate friends but there are
certainly two who can rank as such. To the late Lord
Birkenhead he always listened. To Field-Marshal
Smuts he always listens, and that not merely because
it tickles his fancy to have as a friend and counsellor
one who was once his gaoler. That is not really the
basis of their association. I think that what he sees in
the Field-Marshal is the living embodiment of the
virtues of the British system—a man once in arms
against the British Empire and thereafter its most loyal
supporter. As has already been mentioned, Mr.
Churchill is half American, but in his love for things
British, in veneration for British traditions, and in admiration for British achievements, he is the most
English soul alive. The most un-English thing about
him is his capacity to appreciate foreigners. It could
never be said of him, as Masefield said of one of the
characters in 'Reynard the Fox'—

> 'Two things he failed to understand:
> The foreigner, and what was new.'

You can think your own people have a lot to teach
others without assuming that others have nothing to
teach them. You can love old things without loving

old ways. Mr. Churchill can certainly be moved by the spectacle or memory of majestic events and institutions. The cynic may think that he regards the twentieth century too much through spectacles of the eighteenth. But he can also be moved by very humble and modern things. For example, one of the things which moved him most during the war was the attitude of the people when he passed among them after, and sometimes during, bad raids. 'What an imperial race!' he exclaimed on one occasion when, as he himself told the House of Commons, people emerged from the wreck of their homes to cry 'We can take it!' and also 'Give it 'em back!'

He is, after all, like them himself. All his life he has taken it, and also given it back. He has sought colour in life and he has found it, whether dark or bright. When I seek for a word to sum up the quality of the man, I come back again to 'panache'. That is it. The prayer in history which suits him best is surely the prayer of La Hire: 'Sir God, I pray you to do to La Hire as La Hire would do to you if you were La Hire and La Hire were God.'

The message in history which fits him best is perhaps that which Michael Collins sent on the eve of his assassination, and which many other men in many other contexts have echoed:

'Tell Winston we could never have done anything without him.'

MAXIMS AND REFLECTIONS

CHAPTER I

ON HIMSELF

I have a tendency against which I should, perhaps, be on my guard, to swim against the stream.

At all times, according to my lights and throughout the changing scenes through which we are all hurried, I have always faithfully served two public causes which, I think, stand supreme—the maintenance of the enduring greatness of Britain and her Empire, and the historical continuity of our island life.

On accepting the leadership of the Conservative Party, October 1940.

It must be remembered that Mr. Churchill had throughout his life been unpopular among a large section of that party, and never more so than when he was fighting appeasement.

I now [as Home Secretary in 1911] signed general warrants authorising the examination of all the correspondence of particular people upon a list, to which additions were continually being made. This soon disclosed a regular and extensive system of German-paid British agents. [The field of preparation], once I got drawn in, dominated all other interests in my mind. For seven years I could think of little else . . . all the war cries of our election struggles began to seem unreal. . . . Only Ireland held her place among the grim realities. No doubt other Ministers had similar mental experiences. I am telling my own tale.

The World Crisis.

I am a child of the House of Commons. I was brought up in my father's house to believe in democracy. 'Trust the people' was his message. . . . In

33

my country, as in yours, public men are proud to be servants of the State and would be ashamed to be its masters.

Speech to the American Congress, December 1941.

We shape our dwellings, and afterwards our dwellings shape us.

Speech on rebuilding the House, October 28, 1944.

Looking back with after-knowledge and increasing years, I seem to have been too ready to undertake tasks which were hazardous or even forlorn.

The World Crisis, written in 1923.

There were still in store a few similar tasks for him to undertake.

I am certainly not one of those who need to be prodded. In fact, if anything, I am a prod.

Speech in the House, November 11, 1942.

I cannot help reflecting that if my father had been an American and my mother British, instead of the other way round, I might have got here on my own.

Speech to the U.S. Congress, December 16, 1941.

I feel on both sides of the Atlantic Ocean . . . In my mother's birth city of Rochester, I hold a latch-key to American hearts.

Speech in Rochester, U.S.A., June 1942.

I was happy as a child with my toys in my nursery. I have been happier every year since I became a man. But this interlude of school makes a sombre grey patch upon the chart of my journey.

My Early Life.

In all the twelve years I was at school no one ever

succeeded in making me write a Latin verse or learn any Greek except the alphabet.

My Early Life.

I would make boys all learn English; and then I would let the clever ones learn Latin as an honour and Greek as a treat. But the only thing I would whip them for is not knowing English. I would whip them hard for that.

My Early Life.

I may claim myself to have added the words 'seaplane' and 'flight' (of aeroplanes) to the dictionary.

Thoughts and Adventures.

He spoke nothing but Arabic; I only one word of that language. Still, we conversed fluently. By opening and shutting my mouth and pointing to my stomach, I excited his curiosity, if not his wonder. Then I employed the one and indispensable Arabic word 'Backsheesh'. After that, all difficulties melted away.

The River War.

Be on your guard! I am going to speak in French— a formidable undertaking and one which will put great demands upon your friendship for Great Britain.

Speech in Paris after the Liberation of France.

Hitler, in one of his recent discourses, declared that the fight was between those who have been through the Adolf Hitler schools and those who have been at Eton. Hitler has forgotten Harrow. . . .

Speech at Harrow, December 18, 1940.

You have the songs of Bowen and Howson (whom I remember well as housemasters here) with the music

of John Farmer and Eaton Fanning. They are wonder-
ful; marvellous; more than could be put into bricks
and mortar, or treasured in any trophies of silver or
gold. They grow with the years. I treasure them and
sing them with joy.

Speech at Harrow, November 19, 1942.

It took me three tries to pass into Sandhurst.

My Early Life.

I have been brought up and trained to have the utmost contempt for people who get drunk.

My Early Life.

I resolved to read history, philosophy, economics,
and things like that. . . . Without more ado I got out
the eight volumes of Gibbon's *Decline and Fall of the
Roman Empire.*

My Early Life.

Mr. Churchill explains how, when a subaltern at Bangalore, he began to realise
that polo was not everything.

Twenty to twenty-five! Those are the years!

My Early Life.

I, too, was proud of my prisoner—until we reached
the army. Then it appeared that . . . he was a most
important individual in the employ of the Intelligence
Department who had been spying in Omdurman. . . .
Naturally, several young gentlemen saw fit to be face-
tious on the subject. . . . Reuter's correspondent even
proposed to telegraph some account of this noteworthy
capture. But I prevailed on him not to do so, having
a detestation of publicity.

The River War.

The night was chilly. Colonel Byng and I shared a blanket. When he turned over I was in the cold. When I turned over I pulled the blanket off him and he objected. He was the Colonel. It was not a good arrangement.

At Spion Kop with Colonel Byng—later Lord Byng of Vimy.

'I presume,' Lord Curzon said to me, 'it will not be long before we hear you declaim in the House of Commons!' Though greatly hampered by inability to compose at the rate necessary for public speaking, I was strongly of the same opinion myself.

Great Contemporaries. The occasion was a visit to Curzon as Viceroy in 1896.

I have consistently urged my friends to abstain from reading it.

On Savrola, his first novel and his only one.

Keep cool, men! This will be interesting for my paper.

When the armoured train from Estcourt on which he was travelling as a war correspondent was ambushed by the Boers.

So, at any rate, I had been 'under fire'. That was something. Nevertheless I began to take a more thoughtful view of our enterprise than I had hitherto done.

On first coming under fire in Cuba, 1895.

The President of the Psychical Research Society extracted rather unseasonably a promise from me after dinner to 'communicate' with him should anything unfortunate occur.

My Early Life. On leaving for Kitchener's army in the Soudan.

The best advice I got was from Mr. Henry Chaplin, who said to me in his rotund manner: 'Don't be hurried! Unfold your case! If you have anything to say, the House will listen.'

On the birth-pangs of his maiden speech.

I am very glad the House has allowed me after an interval of fifteen years to lift again the tattered flag I found lying on a stricken field.

Speech in the House, 1901.

Mr. Churchill is referring to his father's fight for economy in the Services, which ended in defeat and resignation. Economy was the text of this, one of the earliest speeches, of his son.

It is easy for an individual to move through those insensible gradations from left to right, but the act of crossing the floor [i.e. changing one's political party] is one that requires serious consideration. I am well informed on the matter, for I have accomplished that difficult process not only once, but twice.

All the years that I have been in the House of Commons I have always said to myself one thing: 'Do not interrupt', and I have never been able to keep to that resolution.

Speech in the House, July 10, 1935.

Don't get torpedoed; for if I am left alone your colleagues will eat me.

Letter to Mr. Lloyd George in 1916, *when latter was proposing to go on a visit to Russia. Mr. Churchill was, at the time, still in bad odour with the Conservatives.*

I found I could add nearly two hours to my working day by going to bed for an hour after luncheon.

My Early Life.

I am finished.

> *To Lord Riddell, on losing his position at the Admiralty in 1915.*

I will never stifle myself in such a moral and intellectual sepulchre.

> *On the Bonar Law Government of 1922, with its policy allegedly reactionary.*

I am without an office, without a seat, without a party, and without an appendix.

> *After his defeat at Dundee in 1922.*
>
> Mr. Churchill had been operated upon for appendicitis just before the contest, and had quarrelled with both the Liberal and Conservative parties over their refusal to continue the Coalition.

I have myself some ties with Scotland . . . ties precious and lasting. First of all, I decided to be born upon St. Andrew's Day—and it was to Scotland I went to find my wife. . . . I sat for fifteen years as the representative of 'Bonnie Dundee', and I might be sitting for it still if the matter had rested entirely with me.

> *Speech on receiving the Freedom of Edinburgh.*
>
> Mrs. Churchill was Miss Clementine Hozier. Mr. Churchill was defeated in Dundee at the General Election of 1922.

I was eleven years a fairly solitary figure in this House and pursued my way in patience; and so there may be hope for the hon. Member.

> *Retort to Mr. Gallacher, the solitary Communist M.P., December 8, 1944. Mr. Churchill was teasing Mr. Gallacher on his failure to gain support in the House.*

I suppose they asked me to show him that, if they couldn't bark themselves, they kept a dog who could bark and might bite.

> *Remark upon being invited by the Chamberlain Cabinet to meet Von Ribbentrop, when the latter was German Ambassador.*

There was a moment . . . of a world aglare, of a man aghast . . . I do not understand why I was not broken like an eggshell or squashed like a gooseberry.

On being run down by a taxi in New York, 1932.

When I was called upon to be Prime Minister, now nearly two years ago, there were not many applicants for the job. Since then perhaps the market has improved.

Speech in the House, January 1942.

It had many defects and teething troubles, and when these became apparent the tank was appropriately rechristened the 'Churchill'. These defects have now been largely overcome.

Speech in the House, July 2, 1942.

I am invited under the threats of unpopularity to victimise the Chancellor of the Duchy [Mr. Duff Cooper] and throw him to the wolves. I say to those who make this amiable suggestion . . . 'I much regret that I am unable to gratify your wishes', or words to that effect.

Speech in the House, January 1942.

It had been sought to make Mr. Duff Cooper, sent on a special mission to Singapore, responsible for the early disasters in the Japanese war. Mr. Churchill has always refused to hear a word against either Mr. Duff Cooper or Mr. Eden, chiefly, I think, because of their revolt against the Chamberlain appeasement policy.

It was my duty as Home Secretary more than a quarter of a century ago to stand beside His Majesty and proclaim his style and titles at his investiture as Prince of Wales. . . . I should have been ashamed if, in my independent and unofficial position, I had not

cast about for every lawful means, even the most forlorn, to keep him on the Throne of his fathers.

Speech in the House of Commons on the abdication of Edward VIII.

The point is that Mr. Churchill had been accused, not openly, but in the
miasmic coulisses of politics, of wanting to form a King's Party with himself at
its head, and to climb back into power on the shoulders of a crisis. This was a
loathsome slander. Mr. Churchill was animated by personal and sentimental
memories, and by them alone.

I was the most miserable Englishman in America
since Burgoyne.

On receiving the news of the fall of Tobruk, June 1942, *when on
a visit to Washington.*

It fell to me in those days to express the sentiments
and resolves of the British nation in that supreme crisis
of its life. That was to me an honour far beyond any
dreams or ambitions I had ever nursed; and it is one
that cannot be taken away.

Verdict on his Premiership.

I regret that I have not been permitted to finish the
work against Japan.

From message after the General Election of 1945.

I do not think any expression of scorn or severity
which I have heard used by our critics has come any-
where near the language I have been myself accustomed
to use, not only orally, but in a stream of written
minutes. In fact, I wonder that a great many of my
colleagues are on speaking terms with me.

Speech in the House, June 25, 1941.

If the worst came to the worst, I might have a shot
at it myself.

*Reply to an Opposition request to name a Minister to speak on behalf
of the Government.*

I have no intention of passing my remaining years in explaining or withdrawing anything I have said in the past, still less in apologising for it.

Speech in the House, April 21, 1944.

If I am accused of this mistake, I can only say with M. Clemenceau on a celebrated occasion: 'Perhaps I have made a number of other mistakes of which you have not heard.

Speech in the House, 1945.

It would be easy for me to retire gracefully in an odour of civic freedom.

Speech to the Conservative Conference, 1946.

I give my opinion. I dare say it will weigh as much as a mocking giggle.

Speech in the House, 1944, *when jeered at for his references to Prince Umberto.*

I will not pretend that, if I had to choose between Communism and Nazi-ism, I would choose Communism. I hope not to be called upon to survive in the world under a Government of either of those dispensations.

Speech in the House, April 14, 1937.

Everybody threw the blame on me. I have noticed that they nearly always do. I suppose it is because they think I shall be able to bear it best.

My Early Life.

When I think of the fate of poor old women, so many of whom have no one to look after them and nothing to live on at the end of their lives, I am glad to have had a hand in all that structure of pensions and

insurance which no other country can rival and which
is especially a help to them.

My Early Life.

The reference is to Mr. Churchill's championship of social insurances almost
from his entry into politics, and to his Widows, Orphans and Old Age Contri-
butory Pensions Act, 1928.

I had a feeling once about Mathematics—that I saw
it all. Depth beyond Depth was revealed to me—the
Byss and the Abyss. I saw—as one might see the
transit of Venus or even the Lord Mayor's Show—a
quantity passing through infinity and changing its sign
from plus to minus. I saw exactly how it happened
and why the tergiversation was inevitable—but it was
after dinner and I let it go.

My Early Life.

CHAPTER II

ON HIS DISLIKES

ON LORD MACAULAY

It is beyond our hopes to overtake Lord Macaulay.
. . . We can only hope that Truth will follow swiftly
enough to fasten the label 'Liar' to his genteel coat-
tails.

Marlborough.

ON THE LATE LORD ESHER

It is remarkable that Lord Esher should be so much
astray. . . . We must conclude that an uncontrollable
fondness for fiction forbade him to forsake it for fact.
Such constancy is a defect in an historian.

*Note on Lord Esher's description of Mr. Churchill's part in the
Antwerp operation.*

ON THE MARGRAVE OF BADEN

His military epitaph for all time must be that the
two greatest captains of the age, pre-eminent and renowned in all the annals of war, rated, by actions more
expressive than words, his absence from a decisive
battlefield well worth fifteen thousand men.

Marlborough.

ON LORD CURZON

His facility carried him with a bound into prolixity;
his ceremonious diction wore the aspect of pomposity;
his wide knowledge was accused of superficiality; his
national pre-eminence was accompanied by airs of
superiority. . . . He aroused both envy and admiration, but neither much love nor much hatred.

Great Contemporaries.

The morning had been golden; the noontide was bronze; and the evening lead. But all were solid and each was polished till it shone after its fashion.

Great Contemporaries.

ON MR. DALTON

The hon. Gentleman is trying to win distinction by rudeness.

On Mr. Dalton's reference to the non-publication of an appeal for a peaceful settlement of the General Strike by the Christian Churches, May 10, 1926.

ON LORD STRABOLGI (THEN LIEUT.-COMMANDER KENWORTHY, M.P.)

His doctrine and his policy is to support and palliate every form of terrorism so long as it is the terrorism of revolutionaries against the forces of law and order.

Speech on the Punjab disturbances, July 8, 1920.

ON RAMSAY MACDONALD

The Government are defeated by thirty votes and then the Prime Minister rises in his place, utterly unabashed, the greatest living master of falling without hurting himself, and airily assures us that nothing has happened.

Speech in the House, January 21, 1931.

I remember, when I was a child, being taken to the celebrated Barnum's Circus, which contained an exhibition of freaks and monstrosities, but the exhibit on the programme which I most desired to see was the one described as 'The Boneless Wonder'. My parents judged that that spectacle would be too revolting and demoralising for my youthful eyes, and I have waited fifty years to see the Boneless Wonder sitting on the Treasury Bench.

Speech in the House, January 28, 1931.

We know that he has, more than any other man, the gift of compressing the largest amount of words into the smallest amount of thought.

Speech in the House, March 23, 1933.

ON LORD CHARLES BERESFORD

He can best be described as one of those orators who, before they get up, do not know what they are going to say; when they are speaking, do not know what they are saying; and, when they have sat down, do not know what they have said.

Speech after his appointment to the Admiralty in 1911. Lord Charles Beresford was a bitter critic of the new broom.

ON COUNT BERCHTOLD

He meant at all costs, by hook or by crook, to declare war on Serbia. In the whole world that was the only thing that counted with him. That was what Germany had urged. That he must have; and that he got. But he got much more, too.

The World Crisis.

ON THE EX-KAISER

The defence which can be made will not be flattering to his self-esteem . . . 'Look at him; he is only a blunderer.'

Great Contemporaries.

It is shocking to reflect that upon the word or nod of a being so limited there stood obedient and attentive for thirty years the forces which, whenever released, could devastate the world. It was not 'his fault'; it was his fate.

Great Contemporaries.

ON BERNARD SHAW

He was one of my earliest antipathies. . . . This bright, nimble, fierce, and comprehending being—Jack Frost dancing bespangled in the sunshine.

He is at once an acquisitive Capitalist and a sincere Communist. He makes his characters talk blithely about killing men for the sake of an idea; but would take great trouble not to hurt a fly.

Great Contemporaries.

If the truth must be told, our British island has not had much help in its troubles from Mr. Bernard Shaw. When nations are fighting for life, when the palace in which the jester dwells not uncomfortably is itself assailed, and everyone from prince to groom is fighting on the battlements, the jester's jokes echo only through deserted halls, and his witticisms and condemnations, distributed evenly between friend and foe, jar the ear of hurrying messengers, of mourning women and wounded men. The titter ill accords with the tocsin, or the motley with the bandages.

Great Contemporaries.

ON LADY ASTOR

She enjoys the best of all worlds . . . She denounces the vice of gambling in unmeasured terms, and is closely associated with an almost unrivalled racing stable. She accepts Communist hospitality and flattery, and remains the Conservative Member for Plymouth.

Great Contemporaries.

ON TROTSKY

He sits disconsolate—a skin of malice stranded for

a time on the shores of the Black Sea and now washed up in the Gulf of Mexico.

He possessed in his nature all the qualities requisite for the art of civic destruction—the organising command of a Carnot, the cold detached intelligence of a Machiavelli, the mob oratory of a Cleon, the ferocity of a Jack the Ripper, the toughness of Titus Oates.

Great Contemporaries.

I must confess that I never liked Trotsky.

Speech in the House, August 2, 1944.

ON LENIN

He alone could have found the way back to the causeway. The Russian people were left floundering in the bog. Their worst misfortune was his birth, their next worst—his death.

The World Crisis.

Mr. Churchill had a certain admiration for Lenin's talents, and is pointing out that his early death took place at the moment when he seemed anxious to curb the worst practical and theoretical excesses of the Revolution.

It was with a sense of awe that they [the Germans] turned upon Russia the most grisly of all weapons. They transported Lenin in a sealed truck like a plague bacillus from Switzerland into Russia.

The World Crisis.

ON PRESIDENT WILSON

The inscrutable and undecided judge upon whose lips the lives of millions hung.

He did not truly divine the instinct of the American people.

First and foremost, all through and last, he was a party man.

The spacious philanthropy which he exhaled upon Europe stopped quite sharply at the coasts of his own country.

The World Crisis.

ON LORD NORTHCLIFFE

. . . at all times animated by an ardent patriotism and an intense desire to win the war. But he wielded power without official responsibility, enjoyed secret knowledge without the general view, and disturbed the fortunes of national leaders without being willing to bear their burdens.

The World Crisis.

ON LORD OXFORD AND ASQUITH

When Lord Fisher resigned in May and the Opposition threatened controversial debate, Asquith did not hesitate to break his Cabinet up, demand the resignation of all Ministers, and the political lives of half his colleagues, throw Haldane to the wolves, leave me to bear the burden of the Dardanelles, and sail victoriously on at the head of a Coalition Government. Not 'all done by kindness'! Not all by rosewater! These were the convulsive struggles of a man of action and of ambition at death-grips with events.

The phrase 'Wait and see' which he had used in peace, not indeed in a dilatory but in a minatory sense, reflected with injustice, but with just enough truth to be dangerous, upon his name and policy.

Great Contemporaries.

He fashioned with deep thought impeccable verses in complicated metre, and recast in terser form classical inscriptions which displeased him.   I could not help much in this!

Great Contemporaries.

Mr. Churchill and Mr. Asquith went together for a holiday in the Mediterranean on the Admiralty yacht. The scion of Balliol proved to have a mind which 'opened and shut smoothly and exactly like the breech of a gun', and Mr. Churchill rather found that the bigger the gun the greater the bore.

ON SIR WILLIAM ROBERTSON

The reader may pass lightly over such incidents as that of General Robertson, who never himself at any time led even a troop in action . . . speaking of the Cabinet as 'poltroons'.

The World Crisis.

ON THE HOUSE OF LORDS

. . . *this* Second Chamber as it is—one-sided, hereditary, unpurged, unrepresentative, irresponsible, absentee.

Speech in the House, June 29, 1907.

I will retort the question of the Leader of the Opposition by another question. Has the House of Lords ever been right?

Speech in the House, June 29, 1907.

ON THE LATE SOCIALIST GOVERNMENT (1931)

After listening to his [Mr. William Graham's] capacious harangue and its immaculate delivery, one would never have thought that the speaker was the representative of an administration which, having reduced this country almost to beggary, had fled from their posts in terror of the consequences which were approaching them.

Speech in the House on the Revised Budget Proposals, September 15, 1931.

ON THE GERMAN ARMY

The deadly, drilled, docile, brutish masses of the Hun soldiery plodding on like a swarm of crawling locusts.

Broadcast on Hitler's invasion of Russia, June 1941

ON PRINCE PAUL OF YUGOSLAVIA

'Prince Palsy.'

Nickname reputed to have been invented when Prince Paul, as Regent of Yugoslavia, was coquetting with the Axis.

ON SIR STAFFORD CRIPPS

Neither of his colleagues can compare with him in that acuteness and energy of mind with which he devotes himself to so many topics injurious to the strength and welfare of the State.

Speech in the House, December 12, 1946.

ON MUSSOLINI

This whipped jackal, who to save his own skin, has made of Italy a vassal State of Hitler's Empire, is frisking up by the side of the German tiger with yelps not only of appetite—that could be understood—but even of triumph.

Speech in the House, April 1941.

I must pay my tribute to Signor Mussolini, whose prestige and authority—by the mere terror of his name —quelled the wicked depredations of these marauders.

Speech in the House on the Nyon Conference, December 21, 1937.

This Conference had agreed to attack submarines which were sinking merchant ships on the way to Spain. The point of the observation is that these submarines were well known to be Italian, though diplomacy was supposed to dictate ignorance of the fact.

The hyena in his nature broke all bounds of decency and even common sense.

Broadcast, November 29, 1942.

ON HITLER

This bloodthirsty guttersnipe.

In broadcast, June 1941.

In North Africa, we builded better than we knew. For this we have to thank the military intuition of Corporal Hitler. We may notice the touch of the master hand. The same insensate obstinacy . . .

Speech to the American Congress, May 1943.

I always hate to compare Napoleon with Hitler, as it seems an insult to the great Emperor and warrior to compare him in any way with a squalid caucus boss and butcher.

Speech in the House, September 1944.

When Herr Hitler escaped the bomb on July 21 he described his survival as providential. I think from a purely military point of view we can all agree with him. Certainly it would be most unfortunate if the Allies were to be deprived in the closing phases of the struggle of that form of warlike genius by which Corporal Schickelgruber has so notably contributed to our victory.

Speech in the House, September 1944.

There must not be lacking in our leadership something of the spirit of that Austrian corporal who, when all had fallen into ruins about him, and when Germany seemed to have sunk for ever into chaos, did not hesitate to march forth against the vast array of victorious nations, and has already turned the tables so decisively upon them.

Speech in the House, October 4, 1938.

This is not merely a case of giving the devil his due. Mr. Churchill was speaking to an audience many of whom could objectively admire Hitler's resuscitation of German might against great odds, and was tempering the wind to these gambolling and still unshorn lambs.

ON MR. GANDHI

It is alarming and also nauseating to see Mr. Gandhi, a seditious Middle Temple lawyer, now posing as a fakir, striding half naked up the steps of the Viceregal palace to parley on equal terms with the representative of the King-Emperor.

ON MR. ANEURIN BEVAN

There is, however, a poetic justice in the fact that the most mischievous mouth in wartime has also become in peace the most remarkable administrative failure.

Speech at Blackpool, October 5, 1946.

There is no one more free with interruptions, taunts, and jibes than he is. I saw him—I heard him, not saw him—almost assailing some of the venerable figures on the bench immediately below him. He need not get so angry because the House laughs at him: he ought to be pleased when they only laugh at him.

Speech in the House of Commons, December 8, 1944.

I should think it hardly possible to state the opposite of the truth with more precision.

Retort in the House, December 8, 1944.

ON MR. DE VALERA

Mr. De Valera, oblivious to the claims of conquered peoples, has also given his croak in this sense. No sooner had he clambered from the arena into the Imperial box than he hastened to turn his thumb down upon the first prostrate gladiator he saw.

De Valera urges recognition of the Italian conquest of Abyssinia, February 4, 1938.

ON THE ITALIAN NAVY

There is a general curiosity in the British Fleet to find out whether the Italians are up to the level they were at in the last war or whether they have fallen off at all.

Speech in the House, June 18, 1940.

ON M. LAVAL

I am afraid I have rather exhausted the possibilities of the English language.

Reply in the House to a request for a 'categorical denunciation' of the French Quisling, September 29, 1942.

CHAPTER III

ON RUSSIA

Russia is a riddle wrapped in a mystery inside an
enigma.

Broadcast, October 1, 1939.

Everybody has always underrated the Russians.
They keep their own secrets alike from foe and friends.

Speech in the House, April 23, 1942.

The giant mortally stricken had just time, with
dying strength, to pass the torch eastward across the
ocean to a new Titan long sunk in doubt who now
arose and began ponderously to arm. The Russian
Empire fell on March 16; on April 6 the United States
entered the war.

The World Crisis.

Lastly, the now inevitable prolongation of the struggle
was destined to prove fatal to Russia. In the war of
exhaustion to which we were finally condemned, which
was indeed extolled as the last revelation of military
wisdom, Russia was to be the first to fall, and in her
fall to open upon herself a tide of ruin in which perhaps
a score of millions of human beings have been engulfed.
The consequences of these events abide with us to-day.
They will darken the world for our children's children. . . . Russia fell to the earth, devoured alive,
like Herod of old, by worms.

The World Crisis.

All sorts of Russians made the revolution. No sort
of Russian reaped its profit. Among the crowds who

thronged the turbulent streets and ante-rooms of Petrograd in these March days, with the resolve 'Change at all costs' in their hearts, were found Grand Dukes, fine ladies, the bitterest die-hards and absolutists; resolute, patriotic politicians; experienced Generals; diplomatists and financiers of the old regime; Liberals and Democrats; Socialists; sturdy citizens and tradesfolk; faithful soldiers seeking to free their Prince from bad advisers; ardent nationalists resolved to purge Russia from secret German influence; multitudes of loyal peasants and workmen; and behind all, cold, calculating, ruthless, patient, stirring all, demanding all, awaiting all, the world-wide organisation of International Communism.

The World Crisis.

In the deepest depth he sought with desperate energy for a deeper. But—poor wretch—he had reached rock bottom. Nothing lower than the Communist criminal class could be found.

On Trotsky, from Great Contemporaries.

Of 'Peter the Painter' not a trace was ever found. He vanished completely. Rumour has repeatedly claimed him as one of the Bolshevik liberators and saviours of Russia. Certainly his qualities and record would well have fitted him to take an honoured place in that noble band.

On the Battle of Sydney Street, from Thoughts and Adventures.

A war of few casualties and unnumbered executions!
Russian Civil War, 1917-19.

They [the Russian villagers] did not yet understand that under Communism they would have a new landlord, the Soviet State—a landlord who would demand a higher rent to feed his hungry cities, a collective land-lord who could not be killed, but who could and would without compunction kill them.

The World Crisis.

There is among us a small but highly intellectual school of thought which reaches its fullest expression in Russia, but also flourishes among some of our smaller neighbours, and which proclaims openly that it is much better for a nation to go through the bankruptcy court and start business again . . . and either to repudiate its debts and start again or pay as much in the £ as it finds convenient by writing its currency down to the necessary figure.

Budget Speech, April 15, 1929.

. . . the old Russia had been dragged down, and in her place there ruled 'the nameless beast' so long foretold in Russian legend.

The World Crisis.

Bela Kun, an offshoot of the Moscow fungus.

The World Crisis.

Bela Kun established a Communist regime in Hungary after the first World War. It lasted only a few months and was overthrown by a counter-revolution.

Here we have a State whose subjects are so happy that they have to be forbidden to quit its bounds under the direst penalties; whose diplomatists and agents sent on foreign missions have often to leave their wives and children at home as hostages to ensure their eventful return.

These weak small States, this long thin line, this *cordon sanitaire* as it was called in France, was four or

five months ago a subject of the deepest anxiety to all
who were concerned with the general problems of
European policy, because when you see how weak they
were, how short of food, how short of money, how deprived of permanent and well-established institutions
or disciplined armies, or organised finances it seemed
almost impossible that, subverted as they were themselves to no inconsiderable extent by the general progress of Bolshevism going on just over their borders,
they should withstand any fierce, general, organised
attack coming from Russia.

Speech in the House, July 29, 1919.

Since the Armistice my policy would have been
'Peace with the German people, war on the Bolshevik
tyranny'. Willingly or unavoidably, you have followed
something very near the reverse. . . . We are now
face to face with the results. . . . Russia has gone
into ruin. What is left of her is in the power of these
deadly snakes.

Memorandum to Mr. Lloyd George, the Prime Minister, in March
1920.

As Secretary of State for War, Mr. Churchill had supplied the White Russian
forces with voluminous munitions, and had supported the Archangel expedition
to the last possible moment. Mr. Lloyd George, on the other hand, did his best
to come to terms with the Bolsheviks.

Trotsky still survives to embarrass the well-meaning
Norwegians, and Lenin's widow waves him signals of
despair faintly distinguishable in the Russian twilight.
Gone are the heroes of the British Socialist Party.
Kameneff, the maker of the first Anglo-Soviet trade
agreement, Zinoviev, of the famous election letter, shot
to rags by Soviet rifles. Tomsky, with his gold watch

from our Trade Union Congress, blows out his brains
to escape his sentence.

From a letter, September 4, 1936.

In this year, the world was astonished to learn that a vast series of State trials
were taking place in Russia in which many politicians and thousands of Army
officers were involved. It has since appeared likely that this purge marked the
defeat and liquidation of pro-Germans.

Russia has pursued a cold policy of self-interest. We
could have wished that the Russian armies should be
standing on their present line as the friends and allies
of Poland instead of as invaders. But that the Russian
armies should stand on this line was clearly necessary
for the safety of Russia against the Nazi menace.

Speech in the House, October 1, 1939.

Mr. Churchill refers to the Russian invasion of Poland in September 1939,
undertaken to prevent Hitler overrunning the whole country.

Any man or State who fights on against Nazidom
will have our aid. Any man or State who marches with
Hitler is our foe.

Broadcast, June 22, 1941.

At four o'clock this morning Hitler attacked and
invaded Russia. All his usual formalities of perfidy
were observed with scrupulous technique.

Broadcast, June 22, 1941.

Mr. Churchill, despite his consistent condemnation of Communism, at once
ranged this country on Russia's side when Hitler invaded her. He had also
repeatedly warned Stalin that the invasion was impending.

Then Hitler made his second great blunder. He
forgot about the winter. There is a winter, you know,
in Russia. For a good many months the temperature
is apt to fall very low. There is snow, there is frost,
and all that. Hitler forgot about this Russian winter.
He must have been very loosely educated. We all

heard about it at school; but he forgot it. I have never made such a bad mistake as that.

Broadcast, May 10, 1942.

What can we do to help Russia. There is nothing that we would not do. If the sacrifice of thousands of British lives would turn the scale, our fellow countrymen would not flinch.

Speech in the House, April 26, 1942.

All through 1942 the Russians and many in other lands were pressing for the opening of a second front in Europe. In this speech Mr. Churchill was explaining that he had not promised to do so, and that the failure to do so was not due to selfishness, but to sound strategy.

We are sea animals, and the United States are to a large extent ocean animals. The Russians are land animals. Happily, we are all three air animals.

Speech in the House, September 8, 1942.

I know of no Government which stands to its obligations, even in its own despite, more solidly than the Russian Government. Sombre indeed would be the fortunes of mankind if some awful situation arose between the Western democracies and the Soviet Union —if the future world organisation were rent asunder and a new cataclysm of inconceivable violence destroyed all that is left of the treasures and liberties of mankind.

Speech in the House on the Crimea Conference.

Mr. Churchill was rebuffing charges of bad faith brought against the Soviet Government's assurances to Poland.

The Russian armies now stand before the gates of Warsaw. They bring the liberation of Poland in their hands. They offer freedom, sovereignty, and independence to the Poles.

Speech in the House, August 2, 1944.

From Stettin, in the Baltic, to Trieste, in the Adriatic, an iron curtain has descended across the Continent. Behind that line lie all the capitals of the ancient States of Central and Eastern Europe—Warsaw, Berlin, Prague, Vienna, Budapest, Belgrade, Bucharest, and Sofia. All these famous cities and the populations around them lie in the Soviet sphere, and all are subject in one form or another not only to Soviet influence, but to a very high and increasing measure of control from Moscow. Athens alone, with its immortal glories, is free to decide its future at an election under British, American, and French observation.

Speech in the House, 1945.

CHAPTER IV

ON HIS LIKES

ON HIS MOTHER

My mother made a brilliant impression upon my childhood's life. She shone for me like the evening star—I loved her dearly, but at a distance.

My Early Life.

ON HIS FATHER

In his speeches he revealed a range of thought, an authority of manner, and a wealth of knowledge, which neither friends nor foes attempted to dispute.

Lord Randolph Churchill.

Lord Randolph's popularity was enhanced by his promotion. Those commanding qualities which the House of Commons had so frankly accepted were now recognised by persons and classes who had hitherto schooled themselves to regard him merely as an unedifying example of irresponsible audacity.

Lord Randolph Churchill.

Would he, under the many riddles the future had reserved for such as he, have snapped the tie of sentiment that bound him to his party, resolved at last to 'shake the yoke of inauspicious stars'; or would he by combining its Protectionist appetites with the gathering forces of labour have endeavoured to repeat as a Tory-Socialist in the new century the triumphs of the Tory-Democrat in the old?

On Lord Randolph, the Tory-Democrat.

That frail body, driven forward by its nervous energies, had all these last five years been at the utmost strain. Good fortune had sustained it; but disaster, obloquy, and inaction now suddenly descended with crushing force, and the hurt was mortal.

Lord Randolph Churchill.

The description is of the consequences of his resignation in 1887, when psychological depression found a dread ally in a lingering and mortal illness.

All my dreams of comradeship with him, of entering Parliament at his side and in his support, were ended. There remained for me only to pursue his aims and vindicate his memory.

My Early Life.

ON HIS NURSE, MRS. EVEREST

My nurse was my confidante . . . [at her death she was] my dearest and most intimate friend during the whole of the twenty years I had lived.

Death came very easily to her. She had lived such an innocent and loving life of service to others, and held such a simple faith, that she had no fears at all and did not seem to mind very much.

My Early Life.

ON MR. WELDON, HEADMASTER OF HARROW

I wrote my name at the top of the page. I wrote down the number of the question '1'. After much reflection, I put a bracket round it thus '(1)'. But thereafter I could not think of anything connected with it that was either relevant or true. . . . It was from these slender indications of scholarship that Mr. Weldon drew the conclusion that I was worthy to pass into Harrow. It was very much to his credit.

My Early Life.

ON THE LATE LORD ROSEBERY

He flourished in an age of great men and small events.

Great Contemporaries.

ON THE LATE JOSEPH CHAMBERLAIN

At the time when I looked out of my regimental cradle and was thrilled by politics he was incomparably the most lively, sparkling, insurgent, compulsive figure in British affairs.

Great Contemporaries.

ON GENERAL GORDON

A man careless alike of the frowns of men or the smiles of woman, of life or comfort, wealth or fame.

The River War.

ON THE LATE LORD MORLEY

Such men are not found to-day. Certainly they are not found in British politics. The tidal wave of democracy and the volcanic explosion of the war have swept the shores bare. . . . The old world of culture and quality . . . was doomed; but it did not lack its standard-bearer.

Great Contemporaries.

John Morley made the greatest impression on Mr. Churchill of all the members of the Liberal Cabinet of 1906. His (Mr. Churchill's) admiration survived even Morley's pacifism.

ON LORD ROBERTS

I have never seen a man before with such extraordinary eyes. . . . The face remains perfectly motionless, but the eyes convey the strongest emotions. Sometimes they blaze with anger, and you see hot yellow fire behind them. Then it is best to speak up straight and clear and make an end quickly.

Ian Hamilton's March

ON A. J. BALFOUR

His aversion from the Roman Catholic faith was dour and inveterate. Otherwise he seemed to have the personal qualifications of a great Pope. . . . He was quite fearless. . . . Poverty never entered his thoughts. Disgrace was impossible because of his character and behaviour.

Great Contemporaries.

He was never excited, and in the House of Commons very hard indeed to provoke. I tried often and often, and only on a few occasions, which I prefer to forget, succeeded in seriously annoying him in public debate.

On A. J. Balfour, from Great Contemporaries.

ON THE BRITISH PEOPLE

Ask what you please; look where you will, you cannot get to the bottom of the resources of Britain. No demand is too novel or too sudden to be met. No need is too unexpected to be supplied. No strain is too prolonged for the patience of our people. No suffering or peril daunts their hearts.

Speech on the Ministry of Munitions, April 1918.

We have not journeyed across the centuries, across the oceans, across the mountains, across the prairies, because we are made of sugar-candy.

Speech to the Canadian Parliament at Ottawa, December 30, 1941.

In all my life I have never been treated with so much kindness as by the people who have suffered most.

One would think one had brought some great benefit to them, instead of the blood and tears, the toil and sweat which are all I have ever promised.

Speech in the House, October 1940.

Mr. Churchill frequently insisted upon visiting the scenes of the worst bombing damage. He was greatly moved by the courage of the victims.

It only remains for me to express to the British peoples, for whom I have acted in these perilous years, my profound gratitude for the unflinching, unswerving support which they have given me during my task, and for the many expressions of kindness which they have shown towards their servant.

Message after defeat at the General Election, July 1945.

ON G. W. STEVENS

The most brilliant man in journalism I have ever met.

My Early Life.

ON THE BOERS

They were the most good-hearted enemy I have ever fought against in the four continents in which it has been my fortune to see Active Service.

My Early Life.

ON LORD KITCHENER

I cannot forget that when I left the Admiralty in May 1915 the first and, with one exception, only one of my colleagues who paid me a visit of ceremony was the overburdened Titan whose disapprobation had been one of the disconcerting experiences of my youth.

The World Crisis.

This was the visit on which Lord Kitchener said to the fallen Minister: 'One thing they cannot take from you—the Fleet was ready!' The 'disapprobation' was in evidence when the young lieutenant of Hussars tried to get attached to the army which Kitchener was leading against the Mahdi. Kitchener disapproved of strings being pulled. As Mr. Churchill says: 'It was a case of dislike before first sight.' The 'disapprobation' had originally been returned, with interest, as witness the following from *The River War*. After accusing the Sirdar (as Lord Kitchener was in 1898) of neglecting his sick and injured and hotly criticising his 'desecration of the Mahdi's tomb', Mr. Churchill remarks that he is 'free to devote to the further service of the State his remarkable talents—talents that will never be fettered by fear and not very often by sympathy'.

ON LORD FISHER

He left me with the impression of a terrific engine of mental and physical power, burning and throbbing in that aged frame.

The World Crisis.

But he was seventy-four years of age. As in a great castle which has long contended with time, the mighty central mass of the donjon towered up intact and seemingly everlasting. But the outworks and the battlements had fallen away, and its imperious ruler dwelt only in the special apartment and corridors with which he had a lifelong familiarity.

The World Crisis.

ON THE LATE LORD LUCAS

His open, gay, responsive nature; his witty, ironical, but never unchivalrous tongue; his pleasing presence; his compulsive smile, made him much courted by his friends, of whom he had many, and of whom I was one. Young for the Cabinet, heir to splendid possessions,

happy in all that surrounded him, he seemed to have
captivated Fortune with the rest.

The World Crisis.

This is a fine example of Mr. Churchill's talent for writing musical English.
Note how the adjective 'responsive' is echoed later by the unusual adjective 'compulsive'.

ON LORD JELLICOE

He was the only man on either side who could lose
the war in an afternoon.

The World Crisis.

The reference is to the huge weight of responsibility falling on the C.-in-C. of
the British Battle Fleet in the First World War. I am not sure, however, that
Lord Jellicoe is rightly included among Mr. Churchill's likes. The tone of
references to him is always explanatory rather than admiring.

ON ADMIRAL EARL BEATTY

His mind had been rendered quick and supple by
the situations of polo and the hunting-field, and en-
riched by varied experiences against the enemy. . . .
I was increasingly struck with the shrewd and profound sagacity of his comments, expressed in language
singularly free from technical jargon.

The World Crisis.

Mr. Churchill rescued Rear-Admiral Beatty, as he then was, from unemployment and the menace of retirement in 1914.

ON IAN HAMILTON

His mind is built upon a big scale, being broad and
strong, capable of thinking in army corps, and, if
necessary, in continents, and working always with
serene smoothness undisturbed alike by responsibility
or danger.

Ian Hamilton's March.

ON RAYMOND ASQUITH

The war which found the measure of so many never

got to the bottom of him, and when the Grenadiers strode into the crash and thunder of the Somme he went to his fate cool, poised, resolute, matter-of-fact, debonair.

Great Contemporaries.

ON MARSHAL FOCH.

He began his career a little cub, brushed aside by the triumphant march of the German armies to Paris and victory; he lived to see all the might of valiant Germany prostrate and suppliant at his pencil tip.

Great Contemporaries.

ON LORD HAIG

Right or wrong, victorious or stultified, he remained, within the limits he had marked out for himself, cool and undaunted, ready to meet all emergencies and to accept death or obscurity should either come his way. . . . The Furies indeed contended in his soul, and that arena was large enough to contain their strife.

Great Contemporaries.

ON GENERAL TUDOR

The impression I had of Tudor was of an iron peg hammered into the frozen ground, immovable.

The World Crisis.

General Tudor commanded a Division of the Fifth Army at the moment of the great German assault on March 21, 1918.

ON M. CLEMENCEAU

He embodied and expressed France. As much as any simple human being, miraculously magnified, can ever be a nation, he *was* France. Fancy paints nations in symbolic animals—the British lion, the American eagle . . . the Gallic cock. But the old Tiger, with his quaint stylish cap, his white moustache and burning eyes, would make a truer mascot for France than any barnyard fowl.

Great Contemporaries.

Clemenceau was called 'the Tiger' from his habit in his younger days of savaging successive Governments in his newspaper or in the Chamber. The sympathy he entertained for Mr. Churchill was exceptional, and extended to few of his own countrymen. It was returned, and Mr. Churchill found in Clemenceau's attitude and speeches in the critical days of 1918, when the Germans were seventy miles from Paris, a model and even a text for his own when the Germans were practically as near London in 1940.

ON GENERAL MANGIN

Bronzed and sombre, thick black hair bristling, an aquiline profile with gleaming eyes and teeth; alive and active, furious, luxurious, privileged, acquisitive . . . reckless of all lives and of none more than his own . . . thundering down the telephone implacable orders to his subordinates and, when necessary, defiance to his superiors, Mangin beaten or triumphant, Mangin the Hero or Mangin the Butcher became on the anvil of Verdun the fiercest warrior-figure of France.

The World Crisis.

ON LORD RAWLINSON

During these vicissitudes he was always the same. In the best of fortunes or the worst, in the most dangerous and hopeless position or on the crest of the wave, he was always the same tough cheery gentleman and sportsman.

The World Crisis.

ON CZAR NICHOLAS II

To the supreme responsible authority belongs the blame or credit for the result. Why should this stern test be denied to Nicholas II? . . . He was neither a great captain, nor a great prince. He was only a true, simple man of average ability, of merciful dispos*i*tion, upheld in all his daily life by his faith in God. But the brunt of supreme decisions rested upon him. At the summit, where all problems are reduced to Yea or Nay, where events transcend the faculties of men, and where all is inscrutable, he had to give the answers. His was the function of the compass needle. War or no war? Advance or retreat? Right or left? Democratise or hold firm? Quit or persevere? These were the battle-fields of Nicholas II. Why should he reap no honour from them? The devoted onset of the Russian armies which saved Paris in 1914; the mastered agony of munitionless retreat; the slowly regathered forces; the victories of Brusiloff—has he no share in those?

The World Crisis.

ON MICHAEL COLLINS

'You hunted me night and day!' he exclaimed. 'You put a price on my head!'

'Wait a minute,' I said. 'You are not the only one!' And I took from my wall the framed copy of the reward offered for my recapture from the Boers. 'At any rate, yours was a good price—£5,000. Look at me—£25 dead or alive. How would you like that?' He read the paper, and as he took it in he broke into a hearty laugh. All his irritation vanished.

This was at the critical phase of the negotiations between the British Government and the Sinn Fein leaders in 1921, which ultimately led to the Irish Treaty; and records the trivial incident which proved to be the turning-point towards success.

ON PHILIP SNOWDEN

He was really a tender-hearted man who would not have hurt a gnat unless his party and the Treasury told him to do so, and then only with compunction. . . . He was a preaching friar with no Superior to obey but his own intellect.

Great Contemporaries.

Mr. Snowden succeeded Mr. Churchill as Chancellor of the Exchequer in 1929. Their exchanges in Parliament were consistently caustic, but behind them was reciprocal respect. I remember well Mr. Churchill's expression—at once disconcerted and touched—when, after one particular duel, Snowden suddenly finished by saying: 'I am really very fond of the right honourable Gentleman, and wish him a Merry Christmas.'

ON THE LATE LORD BIRKENHEAD

He had all the canine virtues in a remarkable degree —courage, fidelity, vigilance, love of the chase.

Some men when they die, after busy, toilsome, successful lives, leave a great stock of scrip and securities, of acres, or factories, or the goodwill of great undertakings. . . . F. E. banked his treasure in the hearts of his friends, and they will cherish his memory till their time is come.

Great Contemporaries.

ON BORIS SAVINKOV

He was that extraordinary product—a terrorist for moderate aims.

Great Contemporaries.

He seemed to be the appointed agent of Russian salvation. A little more time, a little more help, a little more confidence, a few more honest men, the blessing of Providence, and a rather better telephone service— all would have been well!

Great Contemporaries.

ON LLOYD GEORGE

He possessed . . . a power of living in the present without taking short views. Every day for him was filled with the hope and the impulse of a fresh beginning. He surveyed the problems of each morning with an eye unobstructed by preconceived opinions, past utterances, or previous disappointments and defeats. . . . This inexhaustible mental agility, guided by the main purpose of Victory, was a rare advantage. His intuition fitted the crisis better than the logical reasoning of more rigid minds.

The World Crisis.

How could he [Count Metternich] know what Mr. Lloyd George was going to do? Until a few hours before, his colleagues did not know. Working with him in close association, I did not know. No one knew. Until his mind was definitely made up, he did not know himself.

The World Crisis.

In 1911 the German Government sent a gunboat to Agadir, a small Moroccan port, 'to maintain and protect German interests'. It was generally supposed, and has never been disproved, that they wanted to pick a quarrel with France, on the supposition that a British Liberal Government would stand aside. This supposition was rudely dispelled by a speech delivered by Mr. Lloyd George, supposed to be the most pacifist Minister in the Cabinet. The German Ambassador in London was sacked for having misled his Government.

The right hon. Member for Carnarvon Boroughs [Mr. Lloyd George] has distinguished himself upon this subject in a manner which deserves the widest public notice. He said on Saturday: 'You are blessed, for you will not receive, you will give. Every time the lamp illuminates your cottage, and perfumes it, as it used to do in my own days, you will have the feeling that the wick is oozing wealth for Sir Alfred Mond and

Mr. Samuel Courtauld.' That is the contribution to an important public controversy of a man who has been nine years Chancellor of the Exchequer and five years Prime Minister, who, after having held the greatest situation in Europe, looks forward with the utmost gusto to another series of 'Limehouse Nights'.

Budget Debate, May 1, 1928.

ON GENERAL SMUTS

He and I are old comrades. I cannot say there has never been a kick in our gallop. I was examined by him when I was a prisoner of war; and I escaped. But we made an honourable and a generous peace on both sides, and for the last forty years we have been comrades working together.

ON GENERAL BOTHA

His death followed speedily upon his return to his own country, of which in Peace and War, in Sorrow and in Triumph, in Rebellion and in Reconciliation, he had been a veritable saviour. . . .

There was only one [of many distinguished visitors] whom I myself conducted down the great staircase [of the War Office] and put with my own hands into his waiting car.

My Early Life.

ON MR. EDEN

He is the one fresh figure of the first magnitude arising out of a generation which was ravaged by the war.

Speech in the House, February 1938.

ON FIELD-MARSHAL ALEXANDER

He is no glory-hopper.

Saying attributed to Mr. Churchill with reference to the Field-Marshal's self-effacing part in the North African campaigns. The description seems to have been coined—at least, I can find no trace of it in English or American slang—but its meaning is self-evident. It calls up a picture of some bird avidly hopping towards a delicacy.

ON FIELD-MARSHAL MONTGOMERY

This vehement and formidable General—a Cromwellian figure—austere, severe, accomplished, tireless —his life given to the study of war, who has attracted to himself in an extraordinary degree the confidence and devotion of the Army.

Speech in the House, February 1943.

The above is an admirable example of Mr. Churchill's talent for finding the right adjectives. There are generally four, forming, so to say, the four quarters of a canvas. Cf. his description of the Wahabis: 'Austere, intolerant, well armed, and bloodthirsty.' It may be added that he has his favourite adjectives, e.g. 'austere', 'sombre', 'sordid', 'squalid'.

ON LORD LOUIS MOUNTBATTEN

A complete triphibian.

When Lord Louis was appointed to the head of the South-East Asia Command he was given highrank in the Army and Air Force in addition to his rank in the Navy.

ON PRESIDENT ROOSEVELT

That great man whom destiny has marked for this climax of human fortune.

Speech to Canadian Parliament at Ottawa, December 30, 1941.

His love of his own country, his respect for its constitution, his power of gauging the tides and currents of its mobile public opinion—all this was evident. But added to this were the beatings of his generous heart—always stirred to anger and to action by spectacles of aggression by the strong against the weak.

ON MARSHAL STALIN

This great rugged war chief. . . . He is a man of massive outstanding personality, suited to the sombre and stormy times in which his life has been cast; a man of inexhaustible courage and will-power, and a man direct and even blunt in speech, which, having been brought up in the House of Commons, I do not mind at all, especially when I have something to say of my own. Above all, he is a man with that saving sense of humour which is of high importance to all men and all nations, but particularly to great men and great nations. Stalin left upon me the impression of a deep, cool wisdom and a complete absence of illusions of any kind.

Speech in the House, after a visit to Moscow, September 1942.

ON MR. ATTLEE

He is a sheep in wolf's clothing.

Remark attributed to Mr. Churchill in 1945. *The point is that Mr. Attlee, though leader of the Socialist Party and therefore thought by some to be a vehicle for revolutionary ideas, is considered by others to be a mild and colourless personality.*

CHAPTER V

ON WAR

The story of the human race is War. Except for brief and precarious interludes, there has never been peace in the world.

The World Crisis.

The only test by which human beings can judge war responsibility is Aggression; and the supreme proof of Aggression is Invasion.

The World Crisis.

The wars of peoples will be more terrible than those of kings.

Speech in the House on the Army Estimates, 1901.

A single glass of champagne imparts a feeling of exhiliration. The nerves are braced; the imagination is agreeably stirred; the wits become more nimble. A bottle produces a contrary effect. Excess causes a comatose insensibility. So it is with war; and the quality of both is best discovered by sipping.

The Malakand Field Force.

The wholehearted concurrence of scores of millions of men and women, whose co-operation is indispensable, and whose comradeship and brothership upon which the trials and tribulations of modern war can be endured and surmounted . . .

Speech in the House on the outbreak of war, September 3, 1939.

Mr. Churchill, in spite of his campaign against appeasement, immediately acknowledged the moral value of having done everything possible for peace.

War is a game to be played with a smiling face.

O, horrible war! Amazing medley of the glorious and the squalid, the pitiful and the sublime! If modern men of light and leading saw your face closer, simple folk would see it hardly ever!

London to Ladysmith.

War is very cruel. It goes on for so long.

Speech in the House, April 14, 1937.

Before the war [of 1914-18] it had seemed incredible that such terrors and slaughters, even if they began, could last more than a few months. After the first two years it was difficult to believe that they would ever end.

The World Crisis.

An example of the sardonic humour for which the British soldier is famous— 'The first seven years are the worst.'

. . . When young men begged to be allowed to take part in actual fighting, and when the curmudgeons of red tape interposed their veto, I used to brush these objections aside saying: 'After all they are only asking to stop a bullet. Let them have their way.'

My Early Life.

Mr. Churchill is saying that he is not willing to blame young officers for trying to do what he did himself.

It often happens that, when men are convinced that they have to die, a desire to bear themselves well and to leave life's stage with dignity conquers all other sensations.

Savrola, 1900.

You do not rise by the regulations, but in spite of them. Therefore in all matters of active service the subaltern must never take 'No' for an answer. He should get to the front at all costs.
Ian Hamilton's March.

Nothing is more dangerous in wartime than to live in the temperamental atmosphere of a Gallup poll, always feeling one's pulse and taking one's temperature. I see [it said that] leaders should keep their ears to the ground. All I can say is that the British nation will find it very hard to look up to the leaders who are detected in that somewhat ungainly posture.
Speech in the House, September 30, 1941.

With all his faults, right or wrong, he was always for fighting; which is something.
On Goslinga, from Marlborough.

They sound so very cautious and correct, these deadly words. Soft, quiet, purring, courteous, grave, exactly measured phrases in large peaceful rooms. But with less warning cannons had opened fire. . . . So now the Admiralty wireless whispers through the ether to the tall masts of ships, and captains pace their decks absorbed in thought. It is nothing. It is less than nothing. It is too foolish, too fantastic to be thought of in the twentieth century. Or is it fire and murder leaping out of the darkness at our throats, torpedoes ripping the bellies of half-awakened ships, a sunrise on a vanished naval supremacy, and an island well-guarded hitherto, at last defenceless? No, it is nothing. . .

Are you quite sure? It would be a pity to be wrong. Such a mistake could only be made once—once for all.

The World Crisis.

Thoughts aroused by Sir Edward Grey's reply to the German Ambassador that his complaint against Mr. Lloyd George's speech of warning at the time of the Agadir incident was of a tone which 'rendered it inconsistent with the dignity of H.M. Government to give explanations'. The reader may note that this passage may well have been inspired by the Japanese surprise attack on the Russian Fleet in Port Arthur in 1904. It is, in any case, grimly prophetic of Pearl Harbour in 1941.

Consider these ships, so vast in themselves, yet so small, so easily lost to sight on the surface of the waters. . . . Open the sea-cocks and let them sink beneath the surface—half an hour at the most—the whole outlook of the world would be changed. The British Empire would dissolve like a dream . . . mighty provinces, whole Empires in themselves, drifting hopelessly out of control and falling a prey to strangers; and Europe after one sudden convulsion passing into the iron grip of the Teuton and of all that the Teutonic system meant. There would only be left far off across the Atlantic unarmed, unready, and as yet uninstructed America to maintain single-handed law and freedom among men.

Guard them well, Admirals and Captains, hardy tars and tall marines! Guard them well and guide them true.

The World Crisis. Thoughts inspired by the Naval Review at Portland, 1912.

Out of intense complexities intense simplicities emerge.

The World Crisis. On the problems of deploying a fleet.

This is a very dangerous war.

Reply attributed to Mr. Churchill when, as a battalion commander in France, he was reproved by his Divisional General for allowing a part of his trenches to remain in a 'positively dangerous' condition.

There is no principle in war better established than that everything should be massed for the battle.

The World Crisis.

And none more often neglected, as it was in the Dardanelles, which campaign is the context of this remark. Compare Foch's famous principle in 1918: '*Tout le monde a la bataille*', or Napoleon's famous letter to Marmont when collecting his troops before Austerlitz: '*Activité! Activité! Vitesse! Je me recommande a vous.*' And also for the results of the neglect of this principle, compare Hitler's division of his forces after the capture of Rostov in 1942, when he sent part on the drive for Stalingrad and part on the drive into the Caucasus.

Moral force is, unhappily, no substitute for armed force, but it is a very great reinforcement.

Speech in the House, December 21, 1937.

This desert warfare has to be seen to be believed. Large armies, with their innumerable transport and tiny habitations, are dispersed and scattered as if from a pepper-pot over the vast indeterminate slopes and plains of the desert, broken here and there only by a sandy crease or tuck in the ground or an outcrop of rock.

Speech in the House, September 8, 1942.

To hear some people talk, however, one would think that the way to win the war is to make sure that every Power contributing armed forces and branches of these armed forces is represented on all the councils and organisations which have to be set up, and that everybody is fully consulted before anything is done. That is, in fact, the most sure way to lose a war.

Speech in the House, January 27, 1942.

Battles are won by slaughter and manœuvre. The greater the general, the more he contributes in manœuvre, the less he demands in slaughter.

The World Crisis.

But now from the direction of the enemy there came a succession of grisly apparitions; horses spouting blood, struggling on three legs, men staggering on foot, men bleeding from terrible wounds, fish-hook spears stuck right through them, arms and faces cut to pieces, bowels protruding, men gasping, crying, collapsing, expiring. . . . The blood of our leaders cooled. . . . They remembered for the first time that we had carbines.

My Early Life.

The description is of the scene after the charge of the 21st Lancers at Omdurman. Mr. Churchill, who took part, declared that the charge ought never to have been delivered, since the enemy could have been dispersed, as they subsequently were, by carbine fire. The charge was magnificent, but it was not war—as was said of Balaclava.

Antwerp presented a case, till the Great War unknown, of an attacking force marching methodically without regular siege operations through a permanent fortress line behind advancing curtains of artillery fire. Fort after fort was wrecked by the two or three monster howitzers; and line after line of shallow trenches was cleared by the fire of field guns. And following gingerly upon these iron footprints, German infantry, weak in numbers, raw in training, inferior in quality, wormed and waddled their way forward into 'the second strongest fortress in Europe'.

The World Crisis.

The Decisive theatre is the theatre where a vital decision may be obtained at any given time. The

Main theatre is that in which the main armies or fleets are stationed. This is not at all times the Decisive theatre.

The World Crisis.

Mr. Churchill is arguing for attacking the Dardanelles and against concentrating all on the Western Front.

[In] war with any Great Power . . . three Army Corps would scarcely serve as a vanguard. If we are hated, they will not make us loved. If we are in danger, they will not make us safe. They are enough to irritate; they are not enough to overawe. Yet, while they cannot make us invulnerable, they may very likely make us venturesome.

Speech in the House of Commons on the Army Estimates, 1901.

This speech was part of the attack on Brodrick's Army reforms. It was inspired mainly by the desire to pursue in politics his father's line of economy. His argument was 'trust the Navy'. Don't have 'a Navy dangerously weak and an Army dangerously strong'.

The old wars were decided by their episodes rather than by their tendencies. In this (modern) war the tendencies are far more important than the episodes. Without winning any sensational victories, we may win. . . . Germany may be defeated more fatally in the second or third year of the war than if the Allied armies had entered Berlin in the first.

Speech in the House, November 1915.

Nothing in human power could break the fatal chain, once it had begun to unroll. A situation had been created in which hundreds of officials had only to do their prescribed duty in their respective countries to wreck the world. They did their duty.

The World Crisis. On the outbreak of war in 1914.

We also were too late—thirteen years too late; and the lonely man who had looked for help had long since mouldered in a nameless grave. Is this always to be our method of war . . . blunders, follies, bloodshed, an ill-timed or ill-conceived expedition, useless heroism and withdrawal, and then years afterwards a great army striking an overwhelming blow?

The River War.

General Gordon, 'the lonely man', perished when Khartoum fell to the Mahdi in 1885. Kitchener's reconquest of the Sudan was in 1898. The answer to the questions posed in the latter year was, up to 1939, 'Yes'.

The first year—nothing at all; the second year—very little; the third year—quite a lot; the fourth year—all you want.

On a modern munitions programme.

Year after year, and stretching back to an indefinite horizon, we see the figures of the odd and bizarre potentates against whom the British arms continually are turned. They pass in a long procession: The Aknund of Swat; Cetewayo, brandishing an assegai as naked as himself; Kruger, singing a psalm of victory; Osman Digna, the Immortal and Irretrievable; Theebaw, with his umbrella; Lobengula, gazing fondly at the pages of *Truth*; Prempeh, abasing himself in the dust; the Mad Mullah on his white ass; and, latest of all, the Khalifa in his coach of state. It is like a pantomime scene at Drury Lane.

The River War.

Why should we regard as madness in the savage what would be sublime in civilised man? For I hope that if evil days should come upon our own country, and the last army which a collapsing Empire could interpose between London and the invaders were dissolving in rout and ruin, that there would be some—even in these modern days—who would not care to accustom themselves to a new order of things and tamely survive the disaster.

The River War.

The thought is inspired by the courage of the Dervishes in their assaults at Omdurman.

If you want a true picture in your mind of a battle between great modern ironclad ships, you must not think of it as if it were two men in armour striking at each other with heavy swords. It is more like a battle between two eggshells striking each other with hammers.

Speech on the Navy Estimates, 1914.

One lad of about nineteen was munching a biscuit. His right trouser leg was soaked with blood. I asked whether he was wounded. 'No, sir; it's only blood from an officer's head," he answered, and went on eating his biscuit.

London to Ladysmith. The scene is the disaster on Spion Kop.

Of all the grand miscalculations of the German High Command none is more remarkable than the inability to comprehend the meaning of war with the American Union. It is perhaps the crowning example of the unwisdom of framing a war policy upon the computation of material factors alone.

The World Crisis.

There is no place for compromise in war. That invaluable process only means that soldiers are shot because their leaders in council and camp are unable to resolve. In war, the clouds never blow over; they gather unceasingly and fall in thunderbolts.

The World Crisis.

Two things stop the offensive movements of armies: (*a*) Bullets and fragments of shell which destroy the motive power of men, and (*b*) the confusion of the conflict.

The World Crisis.

Pending some new discovery, the only direct measure of defence upon a great scale is the certainty of being able to inflict simultaneously upon the enemy as great damage as he can inflict upon ourselves.

Speech in the House, November 28, 1934.

None should be used until all can be used at once. They should be disposed secretly along the whole attacking front two or three hundred yards apart. Ten or fifteen minutes before the assault these engines should move forward. . . . Nothing but a direct hit from a field gun will stop them.

If artillery is used to cut wire, the directions and imminence of the attack is proclaimed days before-hand. But by this method the assault follows up the wire-cutting almost immediately, i.e. before any reinforcements can be brought up by the enemy or any special defensive measures taken.

Memo on the use of tanks to Sir John French, C.-in-C. B.E.F., November 1915.

The reader should note the date. It is one year before tanks were used at all, and two years before they were used, with real success, for the first time at Cambrai. It is over twenty years before General de Gaulle wrote his famous book on the proper use of tanks, which expounded exactly the same views, and twenty-five years before the Germans put de Gaulle's views into practice in the 'blitzkrieg'—a term, by the way, properly connoting a tank and *not* an air attack.

There never was a moment when it was possible to say that a tank had been 'invented'. There never was a person about whom it could be said 'this man invented the tank'. But there was a moment when the actual manufacture of the first tanks was definitely ordered, and there was a moment when an effective machine was designed as the direct outcome of this authorisation.

The World Crisis.

It was Mr. Churchill who, as First Lord of the Admiralty, gave the first order for eighteen tanks, or 'landships' as they were called, on March 26, 1915. He did not inform either the War Office or the Treasury—an almost unprecedented and certainly unconstitutional reticence, dictated by fear that conventional minds might stifle a great idea.

Compared with Cannae, Blenheim or Austerlitz, the vast world-battle of 1918 is a slow-motion picture. We sit in calm, airy, silent rooms opening upon sunlit and embowered lawns. Not a sound except of summer and of husbandry disturbs the peace; but seven million men, any ten thousand of whom could have annihilated the ancient armies, are in ceaseless battle from the Alps to the ocean.

The awful question of choosing between the Channel ports and keeping the union of the British and French armies did not arise, and Foch's boast 'I will give up neither' was, in fact, made good by British blood. He rode a gallant horse nearly to death; nearly, but not quite.

Great Contemporaries.

The reference is to the refusal of Foch to relieve troops in action. This principle caused great heartburnings among the British High Command during the interval between Foch's appointment as Generalissimo on March 26 and his launching of Mangin's counter-offensive on July 18. Foch was extremely reluctant to reinforce the British front in French Flanders, severely strained by the German offensive of April 9. His 'impression that British troops would stand any test if resolutely called upon was indelible', as Mr. Churchill says elsewhere. In consequence, the British were left wholly to their own resources until April 18, and mainly even after that.

I am doubtful whether the fact that a man has gained the Victoria Cross for bravery as a young officer fits him to command an army twenty or thirty years later. I have noticed more than one serious misfortune which arose from such assumptions. . . . Lord Roberts was an exception.

My Early Life. On Sir Redvers Buller.

As in the shades of a November evening I, for the first time, led a platoon of Grenadiers across the sopping fields . . . the conviction came into my mind with absolute assurance that the simple soldiers and their regimental officers, armed with their cause, would by their virtues in the end retrieve the mistakes and ignorances of Staffs and Cabinets, of Admirals, Generals, and politicians—including, no doubt, many of my own. But, alas, at what a needless cost!

The World Crisis.

My hope is that the generous instincts of unity will not depart from us . . . [so that we] become the prey of the little folk who exist in every country and who frolic alongside the Juggernaut car of war to see what fun or notoriety they can extract from the proceedings.

Speech in the House of Commons, February 22, 1944. Mr. Churchill is suggesting a continuation of the Coalition after the war.

Death stands at attention, obedient, expectant, ready to serve, ready to sheer away the peoples *en masse*; ready . . . to pulverise, without hope of repair, what is left of civilisation. He awaits only the word of command. He awaits it from a frail, bewildered being, long his victim, now—for one occasion only—his Master.

The World Crisis.

He [Mr. Hore Belisha] has spoken of the importance in war of full and accurate intelligence of the movements and intentions of the enemy. That is one of the glimpses of the obvious and of the obsolete with which his speech abounded.

Speech in the House, May 7, 1941.

We were so glutted with victory that in our folly we cast it away.

Speech in the House, June 1940.

This epitaph on the war of 1914-18 was pronounced in the course of an ovation replete with courage when all was black after the fall of France.

A colossal military disaster.
Wars are not won by evacuations.

Speech in the House, June 4, 1940.

These descriptions of Dunkirk are reproduced because they show that Mr. Churchill did not share the hysterical exultation which the evacuation of all but some 30,000 of the B.E.F. from Dunkirk produced. This 'deliverance' had been loudly acclaimed as a victory, simply because it had not been expected that more than a few thousand men could escape.

Your Commission may condemn the men who tried to force the Dardanelles, but your children will keep their condemnation for all who did not rally to their aid.

Speech on the Report of the Dardanelles Commission, March 20, 1917.

Mr. Churchill had lost his office through this affair eighteen months earlier. The view which he here expresses is now universally accepted.

Only faith in a life after death in a brighter world where dear ones will meet again—only that and the measured tramp of time can give consolation.

On war casualties, with special reference to the death of the Duke of Kent.

The problems of victory are more agreeable than those of defeat, but they are no less difficult.

Speech in the House, November 1942.

I have always laid down the doctrine that the redress of the grievances of the vanquished should precede the disarmament of the victors.

Great Contemporaries.

The flying peril is not a peril from which one can fly. We cannot possibly retreat. We cannot move London.

Speech in the House, November 28, 1934.

It is very much better sometimes to have a panic feeling beforehand, and then be quite calm when things happen, than to be extremely calm beforehand and to get into a panic when things happen.

On being asked by Mr. Baldwin not to indulge in panic. Speech in the House, May 22, 1935.

I cannot believe that, after armaments in all countries have reached a towering height, they will settle down and continue at a hideous level. . . . Europe is approaching a climax. I believe that climax will be reached in the lifetime of the present Parliament.

Speech in the House, April 23, 1936.

A splendid moment in our great history and in our small lives.

On the unconditional surrender of Germany.

Might not a bomb no bigger than an orange be found to possess a secret power to destroy a whole block of buildings—nay, to concentrate the force of a thousand tons of cordite and blast a township at a stroke? Could not explosives even of the existing type be guided automatically in flying machines by wireless or other rays, without a human pilot, in ceaseless procession upon a hostile city, arsenal, camp, or dockyard?

Thoughts and Adventures, 1925.

CHAPTER VI

ON BRITAIN AND THE EMPIRE

What kind of people do they think we are?

Speech to the U.S. Congress, December 24, 1941.

Mr. Churchill was referring to the apparent Japanese calculation that Britain would be frightened into surrender.

It is known, alike by peoples and rulers that, upon the whole—and it is upon the whole that we must judge these things—British influence is a kindly and healthy influence and makes for the general happiness and welfare of mankind.

Speech in the House of Commons, 1901.

This was the British Antonine Age. Those who were its children could not understand why it had not begun earlier or why it should ever stop.

Great Contemporaries.

The reference is to the Victorian Age. The Antonine Age was the Roman Empire under the Emperors Antoninus Pius and Marcus Aurelius Antoninus (A.D. 117-160) which Gibbon eulogised as the Golden Age of mankind.

We then refused to embark upon a policy of casting up balances as between the Colonies and the Mother Country, and, speaking on behalf of the Colonial Office, I said that the British Empire existed on the principles of a family and not on those of a syndicate.

On Imperial Preference, May 7, 1907.

Mr. Churchill was a leading opponent of Mr. Joseph Chamberlain's fiscal policy, which included, of course, Imperial Preference.

Cologne Cathedral took 600 years to build . . . sometimes a generation built wrongly, and the next generation had to unbuild, and the next to build again. Still the work went on through the centuries, till at last

92

there stood forth to the world a mighty monument of beauty and of truth to commend the admiration and inspire the reverement of mankind. So let it be with the British Commonwealth.

Speech at Dundee, May 14, 1908.

As things have turned out, the analogy might have been more happily chosen. Ely Cathedral would have served.

The Ministry [Mr. Gladstone's in 1884] were the representatives of the nation in an hour when its spirit was tame and sluggish, its courage and its fortunes low.

The River War. On the failure to relieve General Gordon at Khartoum.

The word 'Empire' is permitted to be used, which may be a great shock to certain strains of intellectual opinion.

Report to Parliament on the meeting of Dominion Premiers, May 24, 1944.

Mr. Churchill is having a hit at those who shy away from the conception of Empire, by pointing out that Empire statesmen glory in the appellation.

Canada is the linchpin of the English-speaking world.

Speech at Mansion House, September 4, 1941, *in the presence of Mr. Mackenzie King.*

Mr. Churchill refers, of course, to Canada's special ties both with the U.S.A. and with Britain.

They [the British] are the only people who like to be told how bad things are—who like to be told the worst.

Speech in the House, June 10, 1941.

The end of 1709 marked the zenith of Britain in Europe, of the Whigs under Queen Anne, and of

Marlborough's career. Thereafter all fell away with
odd rapidity . . . and glorious England turned renegade
before all men.

Marlborough.

To the astonishment of foreign countries and of our
American kinsmen, the spectacle was seen of the King
and Emperor working in the utmost ease and unaffected
cordiality with politicians whose theories, at any rate,
seemed to menace all existing institutions, and with
leaders fresh from organising a General Strike.

Great Contemporaries.

The reference is to King George V and the Socialist Government of 1929-31.
It is only fair to add that most of the leaders in question viewed the General
Strike three years earlier with a mixture of fear and dislike.

The nose of the bulldog has been slanted backwards
so that he can breathe without letting go.

Description of naval strategy in 1914.

The phrase reflects the policy which afterwards developed into keeping the
Grand Fleet at Scapa, where it could deal with any German incursion into the
North Sea without having to maintain a close blockade of German ports.

Once more now in the march of the centuries Old
England was to stand forth in battle against the
mightiest thrones and dominations. Once more, in
the defence of the liberties of Europe and the common right, must she enter upon a voyage of great toil
and hazard across waters uncharted, towards coasts unknown, guided only by the stars. Once more 'the
far-off line of storm-beaten ships' was to stand between
a Continental tyrant and the dominion of the World.

The World Crisis.

Thoughts as the ultimatum to Germany expired, August 4, 1914. The reference is to the blockade of Europe during the Napoleonic Wars.

What of the naked Channel ports—Dunkirk, Calais, Boulogne? 'Fortify Havre,' said Sir John French! One day's general battle, and the sanguine advance and hoped-for counter-stroke had been converted into 'Fortify Havre'!

'It will be difficult to withdraw the troops if the enemy remains in contact'—a disquieting observation. I forget much of what passed between us. But the apparition of Kitchener Agonistes in my doorway will remain with me as long as I live. It was like seeing old John Bull on the rack.

The World Crisis.

On August 24, 1914, a dispatch was received from the C.-in-C. B.E.F. re-counting the course and consequences of the Battle of Mons. It came as a great shock to Kitchener, the Secretary of State for War, and he went round at once to see Mr. Churchill in the latter's room at the Admiralty. Mr. Churchill describes how he saw at once from his appearance that a disaster had occurred.

Shall we by decisive action, in hopes of shortening the conflict, marshal and draw in the small nations in the north and in the south who now stand outside it? Or shall we plod steadily forward at what is immediately in our front? Should our armies toil only in the mud of Flanders, or shall we break new ground? Shall our fleets remain contented with the grand and solid results they have won, or shall they ward off future perils by a new inexhaustible audacity?

The World Crisis. Mr. Churchill is arguing for the project of attacking the Dardanelles.

It cannot be said that the 'soldiers', that is to say the Staff, did not have their way. They tried their sombre experiment to its conclusion. They took all they required from Britain. They wore down alike the manhood and the guns of the British Army almost to destruction. They did it in the face of the plainest warnings and of arguments which they could not answer.

The World Crisis. The reference is to the Battle of Passchendaele.

His [Sir Douglas Haig's] armies bore the lion's share in the victorious advance, as they had already borne the brunt of the German assault. . . . And ever his shot-pierced divisions, five times decimated within the year, strode forward with discipline, with devotion and with gathering momentum.

The World Crisis. On the campaign of 1918.

Frightfulness is not a remedy known to the British pharmacopœia.

Speech in the House, July 8, 1920.

Our aristocracy has largely passed from life into history; but our millionaires—the financiers, the successful pugilists and the film stars who constitute our modern galaxy and enjoy the same kind of privileges as did the outstanding figures of the seventeenth and eighteenth centuries—are all expected to lead model lives.

Marlborough. Mr. Churchill is defending the morals of his ancestor.

We see our race doubtful of its mission and no longer confident about its principles, infirm of purpose, drifting to and fro with the tides and currents of a deeply disturbed ocean. The compass has been damaged. The charts are out of date. The crew have to take it in turns to be captain; and every captain before every movement of the helm has to take a ballot not only of the crew, but of an ever-increasing number of passengers.

Thoughts and Adventures, 1932.

Probably written during the Socialist Government's tenure of office 1929-31, but nevertheless the first shot in the anti-appeasement campaign.

Stripped of her Empire in the Orient, deprived of the sovereignty of the seas, loaded with debt and taxation, her commerce and carrying trade shut out by foreign tariffs and quotas, England would sink to the level of a fifth-rate Power and nothing would remain of all her glories except a population much larger than this island can support.

Speech to the Royal Society of St. George, April 24, 1933 (two months after Hitler came to power), on the dangers of drifting into unilateral disarmament.

The Romans had a maxim: 'Shorten your weapons and lengthen your frontiers.' But our maxim seems to be: 'Diminish your weapons and increase your obligations.' Aye, and 'diminish the weapons of your friends'.

Speech in the House, March 14, 1934.

I dread the day when the means of threatening the heart of the British Empire should pass into the hands of the present rulers of Germany.

Speech in the House, March 8, 1934.

No one can doubt that a week or ten days' intensive bombing attack upon London would be a very serious matter indeed. One could hardly expect that less than 30,000 or 40,000 people would be killed or maimed. The most dangerous form of air attack is the attack by incendiary bombs.

Speech in the House, November 28, 1934.

What a disastrous instrument it [The Treaty of London, 1931] has been, fettering the unique naval knowledge which we possess, and forcing us to spend our scant money on building wrong or undesirable types of ships; and condemning us to send out into deep waters and sink vessels . . . like the four 'Iron Dukes', which would have been invaluable—for convoying fleets of merchant ships to and from Australia and New Zealand in the teeth of hostile cruisers.

Speech in the House, May 22, 1935.

A friend of mine the other day saw a number of persons engaged in peculiar evolutions, genuflections and gestures. . . . He wondered whether it was some novel form of gymnastics, or a new religion . . . or whether they were a party of lunatics out for an airing. They were a Searchlight Company of London Territorials, who were doing their exercises as well as they could without having the searchlight.

Speech in the House, November 12, 1936. Mr. Churchill was arguing for the need for a Ministry of Supply.

We should lay aside every hindrance; and endeavour, by uniting the whole force and spirit of our people, to raise again a great British nation standing up before all the world.   For such a nation, rising in its ancient vigour, can even at this hour save civilisation.

Speech in the House, March 24, 1938.

If you had given the contract to Selfridge's or to the Army and Navy Stores, I believe that you would have had the stuff to-day.

Speech in the House, May 25, 1938, on the disappointing results of three years of rearmament.

They [the British people] should know that there has been gross neglect and deficiency in our defences; they should know that we have sustained a defeat without a war [Munich], the effects of which will travel far with us along our road; they should know that we have passed an awful milestone in our history . . . and that the terrible words have for the time being been pronounced against the Western democracies [Britain and France]: 'Thou art weighed in the balance, and found wanting.' And do not suppose that this is the end. This is only the beginning of the reckoning.

Speech in the House, October 5, 1938.

We have never been likely to get into trouble by having an extra thousand or two of up-to-date aeroplanes at our disposal. . . . As the man whose mother-in-law had died in Brazil replied, when asked how the remains should be disposed of: 'Embalm, cremate, and bury. Take no risks!'

From an article on world affairs, April 28, 1938.

The Royal Navy, especially after the toning-up which it has received, is unsurpassed in the world and is still the main bulwark of our security; and even at this eleventh hour, if the right measures are taken and if the right spirit prevails in the British nation and the British Empire, we may surround ourselves with other bulwarks equally sure, which will protect us against whatever storms may blow.

Speech in the House, March 19, 1936.

For five years I have talked to the House of these matters—not with very great success. I have watched this famous island descending incontinently, recklessly, the stairway which leads to a dark gulf. It is a fine broad stairway at the beginning, but, after a bit, the carpet ends. A little further on there are only flagstones, and, a little further on still, these break beneath your feet.

Speech in the House, March 24, 1938.

The British habit of the week-end and the great regard which the British pay to holidays which coincide with the festivals of the Church is studied abroad.

Speech in the House, April 13, 1939.

Mussolini had just invaded Albania on Good Friday, and Mr. Churchill was arguing that the day had been chosen to ensure British reaction being slow.

I see that Herr Goebbels and his Italian counterpart Signor Gayda have been jeering at us because we have not gone to war with Japan on account of the insults to which Englishmen and New Zealanders have been subjected at Tientsin. They say this shows we are effete. . . . But perhaps thinking men . . . will feel that we may be keeping what strength we have for someone else.

Speech at the Carlton Club, June 29, 1939.

When I warned them [the French Government] that Britain would fight on alone whatever they did, their Generals told their Prime Minister and his divided Cabinet: 'In three weeks England will have her neck wrung like a chicken.' Some chicken! Some neck!

Speech to the Canadian Parliament, December 30, 1941.

I have seen the King, gay, buoyant, and confident when the stones and rubble of Buckingham Palace lay newly scattered in heaps upon its lawns.

Speech at Edinburgh, October 12, 1942.

Look at the mistake that Hitler made in not trying invasion in 1940. We had not, at that time, fifty tanks; we had a couple of hundred field guns, some of them brought out of museums.

Speech, October 31, 1942.

We have the means, and we have the opportunity, of marshalling the whole vast strength of the British Empire and of the Mother Country, and directing these [*sic*] steadfastly and unswervingly to the fulfilmen of our purpose. . . . For each and for all, as for the Royal Navy, the watchword should be 'Carry on and dread nought'.

Speech in the House as First Lord of the Admiralty, December 3, 1939.

Thoughtless, dilettante or purblind worldlings sometimes ask us: 'What is it that Britain and France are fighting for?' To this I answer: 'If we left off fighting you would soon find out.'

Broadcast, March 30, 1940.

I would say to the House, as I said to those who have joined this Government: 'I have nothing to offer but blood, toil, tears, and sweat.' We have before us an ordeal of the most grievous kind. We have before us many, many long months of struggle and suffering.

You ask: 'What is our policy?' I will say: 'It is to wage war by sea, land, and air with all our might, and with all the strength that God can give us: to wage

war against a monstrous tyranny, never surpassed in
the dark lamentable catalogue of human crime.' That
is our policy.

You ask: 'What is our aim?' I can answer in one
word: 'Victory!' Victory at all costs, victory in spite of
all terror, victory however long and hard the road may
be; for without victory there is no survival.

First speech as Prime Minister in the House, May 13, 1940.

I am confident that we shall succeed in defeating and
largely destroying this most tremendous onslaught by
which we are now threatened, and anyhow, whatever
happens, we will all go down fighting to the end.

Speech in the House, September 17, 1940.

If we can stand up to him [Hitler], all Europe may
be free and the life of the world may move forward into
broad, sunlit uplands. But if we fail, then the whole
world, including the United States, including all that
we have known and cared for, will sink into the abyss
of a new Dark Age made more sinister, and perhaps
more protracted, by the lights of perverted science. Let
us therefore brace ourselves to our duties, and so bear
ourselves that, if the British Empire and its Commonwealth last for a thousand years, men will say: 'This
was their finest hour.'

Speech in the House, June 18, 1940—*the day of the French
capitulation.*

We shall not flag or fail. We shall go on to the end.
We shall fight in France, we shall fight on the seas and
oceans, we shall fight with growing confidence and
growing strength in the air. We shall defend our island,
whatever the cost may be. We shall fight on the beaches,

we shall fight on the landing-grounds, we shall fight in the fields and in the streets, we shall fight in the hills. We shall never surrender; and even if, which I do not for a moment believe, this island or a large part of it were subjugated and starving, then our Empire beyond the seas, armed and guarded by the British Fleet, would carry on the struggle, until, in God's good time, the New World, with all its power and might, steps forth to the rescue and liberation of the old.

Speech in the House, June 4, 1940.

Nobody who heard it can ever forget this passage. It set the House of Commons in a roar. There is a story, told in Odette Kahn's *And Hell Followed After*, that when Mr. Churchill was compelled to pause by the cheers, he added, under cover of the noise: 'And beat the asterisks over the head with bottles! That's all we've got.' *Si non e vero, e ben trovato.*

We are told that Herr Hitler has a plan for invading the British Isles. This has often been thought of before. When Napoleon lay at Boulogne for a year with his flat-bottomed boats and his Grand Army, he was told by someone: 'There are bitter weeds in England.' There are certainly a great many more of them since the British Expeditionary Force returned.

Speech in the House, after Dunkirk, June 4, 1940.

We shall not fail or falter; we shall not weaken or tire. Neither the sudden shock of battle nor the long-drawn trials of vigilance and exertion will wear us down. Give us the tools, and we will finish the job.

Broadcast address, February 9, 1941.

Mr. Churchill was answering certain American critics who thought Britain's continuance of the war was hopeless.

Singapore has fallen . . . other dangers gather about us. . . . This, therefore, is one of those moments when the British race and nation can show the sheer quality of their genius. This is one of those moments when they can draw from the heart of misfortunes the vital impulses of victory.

Broadcast, February 15, 1942.

We are no longer alone. We are in the midst of a great company. Three-quarters of the human race are now moving with us. The whole future of mankind may depend upon our action and upon our conduct. So far we have not failed. We shall not fail now.

Broadcast, February 15, 1942.

We shall go forward together. The road upward is strong. There are upon our journey dark and dangerous valleys through which we have to make and fight our way. But it is sure and certain that if we persevere, and we shall persevere, we shall come through these dark and dangerous valleys into a sunlight broader and more genial and more lasting than mankind has ever known.

Speech at Leeds, May 16, 1942.

Here in this strong City of Refuge which enshrines the title-deeds of human progress and is of deep consequence to Christian civilisation . . . we await undismayed the impending assault. Perhaps it will come to-night. Perhaps it will come next week. Perhaps it will never come. We must show ourselves equally capable of meeting a sudden violent shock or (what is perhaps a harder test) a protracted vigil. But be the ordeal sharp, or long, or both, we shall seek no terms, we shall tolerate no parley. We may show mercy— we shall ask for none.

Broadcast, July 14, 1940.

If the lull is to end, if the storm is to renew itself, London will be ready, London will not flinch! . . You [Hitler] do your worst, and we will do our best

Speech at L.C.C. Luncheon, July 14, 1941.

Look at the Londoners, the Cockneys, look at what they have stood up to! Grim and gay with their cry 'We can take it!' and their wartime mood of 'what is good enough for anybody is good enough for us'.

Speech to Canadian Parliament, December 30, 1941.

Never in the field of human conflict was so much owed by so many to so few.

Speech in the House, August 20, 1940.

This is the famous tribute to the fighter pilots in the Battle of Britain. Lord Dowding, then C.-in-C. Fighter Command, had assured the Government that his men could bring down four to one over enemy territory and six or seven to one over Britain. They rather bettered his word.

Undoubtedly this process means that these two great organisations of the English-speaking democracies—the British Empire and the United States—will have to be somewhat mixed up together in some ot their affairs for mutual and general advantage. For my own part, looking out upon the future, I do not view the process with any misgivings. I could not stop it if I wished—no one can stop it. Like the Mississippi, it just keeps rolling along. Let it roll! Let it roll on in full flood, inexorable, irresistible, benignant, to broader lands and better days.

Speech in the House, August 20, 1940.

The reference is to the American agreement to hand over fifty destroyers in return for long leases of certain bases in British Colonial territory.

We shall not fail; and then, some day, when children ask 'What did you do to win this inheritance for us and to make our name so respected among men?' one will say: 'I was a fighter pilot', another will say: 'I was in the submarine service', another: 'I marched with the Eighth Army', a fourth will say: 'None of you could have lived without the convoys and the merchant seamen', and you in your turn will say, with equal pride and with equal right: 'We cut the coal.'

Speech to coalowners and miners, October 31, 1942.

The bright gleam has caught the helmets of our soldiers, and warmed and cheered all our hearts.

Speech at the Mansion House, November 10, 1942.

This speech was made just after the Anglo-American landings in French North Africa and when victory at El Alamein was just declaring itself. As Mr. Churchill said later in the same speech: 'This is not the end. It is not even the beginning of the end; but it is, perhaps, the end of the beginning.'

Historians may explain Tobruk. The Eighth Army has done better; it has avenged it.

Speech in the House, November 11, 1942.

The fall of Tobruk during the retreat to Alamein after defeat at Gazala in 1942 was a terrible shock—the greater because the place had held out for nine months in 1941. The 'avenging' was the victory at Alamein, just before this speech.

The dawn of 1943 will soon loom red before us, and we must brace ourselves to cope with the trials and problems of what must be a stern and terrible year. We do so with the assurance of ever-growing strength, and we do so as a nation with a strong will, a bold heart, and a good conscience.

Broadcast, November 29, 1942.

A quarter of a century ago . . . the House, when it heard . . . the armistice terms, did not feel inclined for debate or business, but desired to offer thanks to

Almighty God, to the Great Power which seems to shape and design the fortunes of nations and the destiny of man; and I therefore . . . move 'That the House do now attend at the Church of St. Margaret, Westminster, to give humble and reverent thanks to Almighty God for our deliverance from the threat of German domination'. This is the identical motion which was moved in former times.

Speech in the House on the German surrender, May 8, 1945.

God bless you all! This is *your* victory! . . . Everyone, man or woman, has done their best. Neither the long years nor the dangers, nor the fierce attacks of the enemy, have in any way weakened the independent resolve of the British nation. God bless you all!

From a balcony in Whitehall, May 8, 1945.

Once again the British Commonwealth and Empire emerges safe, undiminished, and united from a mortal struggle. Monstrous tyrannies which menaced our life have been beaten to the ground in ruin, and a brighter radiance illumines the Imperial Crown than any which our annals record. The light is brighter because it comes not only from the fierce but fading glow of military achievements . . . but because there mingle with it in mellow splendour the hopes, joys, and blessings of almost all mankind. This is the true glory, and long will it gleam upon our forward path.

Speech in the House after news of the Japanese collapse, August 15, 1945.

Neither the sure prevention of war nor the continuous use of world organisation will be gained without . . . the fraternal association of the English-speaking peoples. This means a special relationship between the British Commonwealth and Empire and the United States. . . . Eventually there may come principles of common citizenship, but that we may be content to leave to destiny, whose outstretched arm so many of us can clearly see. I feel eventually this will come.

Speech at Fulton, Missouri, March 3, 1946.

We mean to hold our own. I have not become the King's First Minister in order to preside over the liquidation of the British Empire.

Speech at the Mansion House, November 10, 1942.

Mr. Churchill was speaking of war aims—which had been, curiously enough, a favourite topic of conversation when we looked like losing the war, as part of the same mentality which thought the enemy would be persuaded into surrender by pamphlet raids. Mr. Churchill always refused to encourage this irrelevance, but he pointed out in this speech that we coveted nothing of anybody else's, though we meant 'to hold our own'. It is startling to remember that this modest warning was made the text for bitter charges of Imperialism.

How many political Flibbertigibbets are there not running up and down the land calling themselves the people of Great Britain, and the social democracy, and the masses of the nation!

Speech in Glasgow, October 11, 1906.

CHAPTER VII

ON INDIA

If the Viceroys and Governments of India in the past had given half as much attention to dealing with the social conditions of the masses of the Indian people as they have to busying themselves with negotiating with unrepresentative leaders of the political classes for constitutional changes—if they had addressed themselves to the moral and material problems which are at the root of Indian life, I think it would have been much better for the working folk of Burnley and Bombay, of Oldham and Ahmadabad.

Speech in the House, July 9, 1931.

The author of the *Indian Polity* asserts that the day will come when British and native officers will serve together in ordinary seniority and on the same footing. I do not myself believe that this is possible, but if it should ever come to pass, the way will have been prepared on the polo grounds.

The Malakand Field Force.

The above two quotations epitomise Mr. Churchill's attitude towards India. He conceives of the British position as that of a permanent trusteeship; but the trustees must behave in a most gentlemanly fashion towards their wards.

However we may dwell upon the difficulties of General Dyer during the Amritsar riots, upon the anxious and critical situation in the Punjab, upon the dangers to Europeans throughout that province, upon the long delays which have taken place in reaching a decision about this officer, upon the procedure that was at this point or at that point adopted, however we may dwell upon all this, one tremendous fact stands out—I mean the slaughter of nearly 400 persons and the wounding of probably three or four times as many, at the Jallianwallah Bagh on April 13.

Speech in the House, July 8, 1920.

. . . after 379 persons, which is about the number gathered together in this Chamber to-day, had been killed, and when most certainly 1,200 or more had been wounded, the troops, at whom not even a stone had been thrown, swung round and marched away. . . . I do not think it is in the interests of the British Empire or of the British Army for us to take a load of that sort for all time upon our backs. We have to make it absolutely clear, some way or other, that this is not the British way of doing business.

Speech in the House, July 8, 1920.

Above all, it must be made plain that the British nation has no intention of relinquishing its mission in India or of failing in its duty to the Indian masses, or of parting with its supreme control in any of the essentials of peace, order, and good government.

Speech to the Indian Empire Society, February 12, 1930.

It makes me sick when I hear the Secretary of State saying of India 'she will do this and she will do that'. India is an abstraction. . . . India is no more a political personality than Europe. India is a geographical term. It is no more a united nation than the Equator.

Speech at the Albert Hall, March 18, 1931.

What spectacle could be more sorrowful than that of this powerful country casting away with both hands . . the great inheritance which centuries have

gathered? . . . It is a hideous act of self-mutilation, astounding to every nation of the world.
Speech at the Albert Hall, March 18, 1931.

What are the facts in India? We are told that the opinion of India has changed. But the facts of India have not changed. They are immemorial. The political classes of India are a mere handful compared to the population. The Western ideas they have gathered and reproduced have no relation whatever to the life and thought of India. The vast majority can neither read nor write. There are at least seventy different races and even more numerous religions and sects in India, many of them in a state of antagonism—
    'Our rule in India,' said Lord Randolph Churchill, 'is, as it were, a sheet of oil spread out over and keeping free from storms a vast and profound ocean of humanity.'
Speech to the Indian Empire Society, February 12, 1930.

The Sikh is the guardian of the marches. He was originally invented to combat the Pathan.
The Malakand Field Force.

Except at harvest-time, when self-preservation enjoins a temporary truce, the Pathan tribes are always engaged in private or public war. The life of the Pathan is thus full of interest.
The Malakand Field Force.

These Brahmins, who mouth and patter the principles of Western Liberalism and pose as philosophic and democratic politicians, are the same Brahmins who deny the primary rights of existence to nearly sixty

millions of their own fellow countrymen whom they
call 'untouchables'. . . . They consider themselves
contaminated even by their approach. And then, in a
moment they turn round and begin chopping logic
with John Stuart Mill or pleading the rights of man
with Jean Jacques Rousseau.

Speech at the Albert Hall, March 18, 1931.

There can be no doubt, therefore, that the departure
of the British from India, which Mr. Gandhi advocates,
and which Mr. Nehru demands, would be followed
first by a struggle in the North and thereafter by a
reconquest of the South by the North and of the Hindus
by the Moslems. This danger has not escaped the
crafty foresight of the Brahmins. It is for that reason
that they wish to have control of a British army, or
failing that, a white army of janissaries officered, as Mr.
Gandhi has suggested, by Germans or other Europeans.

Speech at the Albert Hall, March 18, 1931.

The far-reaching extensions of self-government with
which Mr. Montagu's name is associated were a bold
experiment. They have not succeeded. The ten years
which have passed have been years of failure. Every
service which has been handed over to Indian administration has deteriorated.

Speech to the Indian Empire Society, February 12, 1930.

The reference is to the Montagu-Chelmsford Reforms devised in 1919 by
Mr. Edwin Montagu, Secretary of State for India, and Lord Chelmsford, the then
Viceroy. Broadly speaking, they effected a certain measure of provincial autonomy
with certain services administered by Indian Ministers.

We now look after them by means of British officials
on fixed salaries who have no axe to grind, who make
no profit out of their duties, who are incorruptible, who

are impartial between races, creeds and classes, and who are directed by a Central Government which in its turn is controlled by the British Parliament based on twenty-nine million electors. It is now proposed to transfer these British responsibilities to an electorate comparatively small and almost entirely illiterate.

On the I.C.S. Speech to the West Sussex Conservative Association, February 23, 1931.

The reason why, in my judgment, Lord Irwin, for all his virtue and courage, has not succeeded in India as he deserved to, is that he has been proceeding upon a wrong mental theme. His attitude towards India has throughout been an apology. He has not shown sufficient confidence in the indispensable work which our country has done, and is doing, for India, or in British resolution that it shall not be interrupted or destroyed. That is the sole foundation upon which the peaceful and successful administration of India can be based.

Speech at Manchester, January 30, 1931.

Lord Irwin (afterwards Lord Halifax) was Viceroy of India during the period when the revision of the Government of India Act, 1920, was under consideration and the next step towards self-government was to be taken. His prolonged negotiations with Mr. Gandhi and the Congress Party were marked by an infinite patience on his part which Mr. Churchill thought excessive.

I am against this surrender to Gandhi. I am against these conversations and agreements between Lord Irwin and Mr. Gandhi. Gandhi stands for the expulsion of Britain from India. Gandhi stands for the permanent exclusion of British trade from India. Gandhi stands for the substitution of Brahmin domination for British rule in India. You will never be able to come to terms with Gandhi.

Speech at the Albert Hall, March 18, 1931.

If in the sacrifice of every British interest and of all the necessary safeguards and means of preserving peace and progress in India you came to terms with Gandhi, Gandhi would at that selfsame moment cease to count any more in the Indian situation. Already Nehru, his young rival in the Indian Congress, is preparing to supersede him the moment that he has squeezed his last drop from the British lemon.

Speech at the Albert Hall, March 18, 1931.

Our right and our power to restrict Indian constitutional liberties are unchallengeable. Our obligation to persevere in associating the peoples of India with their own government is undoubted. We are free to call a halt. We are free, for the time being, to retrace our steps, to retire in order to advance again.

Speech to Indian Empire Society, February 12, 1930.

A Commission under Sir John Simon (now Lord Simon) was sent to India to report on the constitutional changes shown to be desirable by the working of the Act of 1920. Mr. Churchill was pointing out that the Commission was not bound to recommend advances. In fact, it did recommend advances mainly in the direction of greater provincial autonomy. Its proposals were rejected by the Congress Party, and the British Government called a Round Table Conference to discuss the Report. These discussions resulted in large extensions of the proposals of the Report, but not in agreement. The Government thereupon framed a new Act, going beyond the Report. Mr. Churchill took the view that the proposals of the Report were an absolute maximum.

We believe that the next forward step is the development of Indian responsibility in the provincial government of India. Efforts should be made to make them more truly representative of the real needs of the people. Indians should be given ample opportunities to try their hand at giving capable government in the provinces; and meanwhile the central Imperial executive, which is the sole guarantee of impartiality between races, creeds, and classes, should preserve its sovereign power intact, and allow no derogation from its responsibility to Parliament.

Speech at the Albert Hall, March 18, 1931.

Can there be a worse way of dealing with so grave a problem? Here for weeks all the foundations of British power in India have been laid bare, and every principle has been treated as an open question. The orb of power has been dangled before the gleaming eyes of excitable millions and before the powerful forces of implacable hostility with whom we have, as is well known, to cope in India, while at the same time the background, treated as if they were matters of machinery, are those series of formidable reservations and conditions.

Speech at the Round Table Conference on India, January 26, 1931.

How will the British nation feel about all this? I am told that they do not care. I am told that from one quarter or another they are all worried by unemployment or taxation or absorbed in sport and crime news. The great liner is sinking in a calm sea. One bulkhead after another gives way; one compartment after another is bilged; the list increases; she is sinking; but the captain and the officers and the crew are all in the saloon dancing to the jazz band. But wait till the passengers find out what is their position.

Speech in the House, January 26, 1931.

Mr. Churchill was arguing that the proposals of the Round Table Conference would lead to a complete severance between Britain and India.

Already Mr. Gandhi moves about surrounded by a circle of wealthy men, who see at their finger-tips the acquisition of an Empire on cheaper terms than were ever yet offered in the world. Sir, the Roman senator, Didius Julianus, was dining in a restaurant when they told him that the Prætorian Guard had put the Empire up to auction and were selling it in the ditch in their camp; he ran out, and, according to Gibbon, bought it for £200 sterling per soldier. That was fairly cheap; but the terms upon which the Empire is being offered to this group surrounding Mr. Gandhi are cheaper still.

Speech in the House, March 12, 1931.

Where there have been differences between Indians and Great Britain, some adjustment has been made by Great Britain giving way; but as to differences between Indians themselves, there has not been one concession, not one difficulty has been solved or surmounted. Nevertheless, on we go, moving slowly, in a leisurely manner, jerkily onwards, towards an unworkable conclusion, crawling methodically towards the abyss which we shall reach in due course.

Speech in the House, July 9, 1931.

You will ask me what, then, are we to make of our promises of Dominion status and responsible government. Surely we cannot break our word! There I agree. The formal, plighted word of the King-Emperor is inviolable. It does not follow, however, that every Socialist jack-in-office can commit this great country by his perorations. . . . Except as an ultimate visionary goal, Dominion status like that of Canada or Australia is not going to happen in India in any period which we can even remotely foresee.

Speech at Manchester, January 30, 1931.

Meanwhile, as if to strike a note of realism to Pandits, Mahatmas, and those who now claim to speak for the helpless Indian masses, the Frontier is astir; and British officers and soldiers are giving their lives to hold back from the cities and peacetime wealth of India the storm of Pathan inroad and foray.

Letter, April 16, 1937.

The situation in India on the outbreak of war in 1939 was that Provincial Governments were functioning, but no progress had been made towards the formation of a Federal Government of All-India. When the Japanese joined in the war and advanced to the gates of India the attitude of the Congress Party, dominated by Mr. Gandhi, was that the British should quit India and only passive resistance be offered to the Japanese. This attitude and particularly its practical interpretation as the immediate production of chaos behind the front, received little active support from Indians. Nevertheless, Mr. Churchill's Government resolved to try to come to terms with Congress and dispatched Sir Stafford Cripps to India in March 1942. He offered a self-governing Dominion status, to become effective immediately after the war. At Mr. Gandhi's instigation, Congress after much hesitation rejected this offer. Mr. Gandhi and other Congress leaders, having continued their efforts to frustrate the successful conduct of the war, were interned. Mr. Churchill thereupon made a statement that the Cripps offer was still open and constituted settled British policy.

These principles stand in their full scope and integrity. No one can add anything to them, and no one can take anything away. The good offices of Sir Stafford Cripps were rejected by the Indian Congress Party. This, however, does not end the matter. The Indian Congress Party . . . does not represent the majority of the people of India. . . . It is a political organisation built around a party machine and sustained by certain manufacturing and financial interests. Outside that party and fundamentally opposed to it are the 90,000,000 Moslems in British India; the 50,000,000 Depressed Classes . . . and the 95,000,000 subjects of the princes of India. . . . Upwards of a million Indians have volunteered to serve the cause of the United Nations. . . . In these last two months, when

Congress has been measuring its strength against the Government of India, more than 140,000 new volunteers for the Army have come forward in loyal allegiance to the King-Emperor, thus surpassing all records, in order to defend their native land.

Statement in the House, September 10, 1942.

All sorts of greedy appetites have been excited, and many itching fingers are stretching and scratching at the vast pillage of a derelict Empire.

Speech at the Albert Hall, March 18, 1931.

They are making arrangements that the greatest bluff, the greatest humbug, and the greatest betrayal shall be followed by the greatest ramp. Nepotism, back-scratching, graft, and corruption in every form will be the handmaids of a Brahmin domination.

Speech at the Albert Hall, March 18, 1931.

We wonder whether the traveller shall some day inspect, with unconcerned composure, the few scraps of stone and iron which may indicate the British occupation of India. . . . Yet perhaps, if that unborn critic of remote posterity would remember that 'in the days of the old British' the rice crop had been more abundant, the number of acres under cultivation greater, the population larger, and the death-rate lower, than at any time in the history of India—we should not be without a monument more glorious than the pyramids.

The Malakand Field Force.

CHAPTER VIII

ON FOREIGNERS

No people in the world has received so much verbal sympathy and so little practical support as the Boers. If I were a Boer fighting in the field—and if I were a Boer I hope I should be fighting in the field—I would not allow myself to be taken in by any message of sympathy.

Maiden speech in the House of Commons, February 18, 1901.

This sentiment was viewed with horror by the Conservative Government and was the first step towards a change of party. Mr. Churchill, like many natural soldiers, is constitutionally unable to refrain from acknowledging good qualities in his enemies. Later in the speech he urged that 'the small independence [of the Boers] must be merged in the larger liberties of the British Empire', and spoke of them as 'a brave and enduring foe'. He was able to translate this advocacy into action as a member of the Liberal Government which passed the Union of South Africa Act.

'What can you expect', was the answer characteristic of the Boer—the privileged of God—'from fighting on a Sunday?'

Ian Hamilton's March. The scene is the disaster at Majuba, when Ian Hamilton remarked to a Boer: 'This is a bad day for us.'

One thought to find the President [Kruger]—stolid old Dutchman—seated on his stoep, reading his Bible and smoking a sullen pipe. But . . . on the Friday preceding the British occupation he left the capital . . . taking with him a million pounds in gold, and leaving behind him a crowd of officials clamouring for pay, and far from satisfied with the worthless cheques they had received.

Ian Hamilton's March. The scene is the fall of Pretoria, capital of the Transvaal.

An immense responsibility rests upon the German

119

people for this subservience to the barbaric idea of
autocracy.   This is the gravamen [of the charge]
against them in history—that, in spite of all their
brains and courage, they worship Power, and let themselves be led by the nose.

Great Contemporaries.

Ah! foolish—diligent Germans, working so hard,
thinking so deeply . . . poring over long calculations,
fuming in new-found prosperity, discontented amid the
splendour of mundane success, how many bulwarks to
your peace and glory did you not, with your own hands,
successively tear down!

The World Crisis.

It has often been argued that if Germany had not gone to war in 1914 she
would have become predominant in the world by peaceful means.

He said people were trying to ring Germany round
and put her in a net. . . . I said, how could she be
netted when she had an alliance with two other first-
class Powers, Austria-Hungary and Italy? *We* had
often stood quite alone for years at a time without
getting flustered.

The World Crisis.

Plus ça change, plus c'est la même chose.' These words by Count Metter nich
German Ambassador in 1911, were often echoed by Hitler.

There was the man who fired the shots that killed
the Archduke and his wife at Sarajevo [Princip].   There
was the man who, deliberately accepting the risk of a
world war, told the Austrian Emperor that Germany
would give him a free hand against Serbia and urged
him to use it [the ex-Kaiser].   There was the man who
framed and launched the ultimatum to Serbia [Berch-
told].

The World Crisis. On responsibility for the war of 1914-18.

Alone upon his rocky pinnacle from which the tides of time had sunk, this venerable, conscientious functionary continued in harness, pulling faithfully at the collar, mostly in the right direction, until the last gasp.

The World Crisis. On the Emperor Francis Joseph.

There are a few points on which I am not convinced. Of these, the greatest is the question of the use of submarines to sink merchant vessels. I do not believe this would ever be done by a civilised Power.

Memo to Lord Fisher, January 1, 1914.

It seems difficult now to believe that this was the overwhelming naval opinion before 1914.

To steam at full speed or at a high speed for any length of time on any quest was to use up his life rapidly. He was a cut flower in a vase; fair to see, yet bound to die, and to die very soon if the water was not constantly renewed.

The World Crisis.

On Admiral Von Spee between the battles of Coronel and the Falkland Islands.

Of course, there never was a German submarine in Scapa. . . . At the very end of the war, in November 1918, after the mutiny of the German Fleet, a German submarine manned entirely by officers seeking to save their honour, perished in a final desperate effort.

The World Crisis.

It was the fateful weakness of the German Empire that its military leaders, who knew every detail of their profession and nothing outside it, considered themselves and became arbiters of the whole policy of the State. In France, throughout the war, even in its darkest and most convulsive hours, the civil Government, quivering to its foundations, was nevertheless supreme. . . .

In England Parliament was largely in abeyance. . . . But there existed a strong political caste and hierarchy which, if it chose to risk its official existence, could grapple with the 'brass hats'. In the United States, the civil element was so overwhelmingly strong that its main need was to nurture and magnify the unfledged military champions.

Thoughts and Adventures.

The Battle of Tannenberg inaugurated the memorable partnership of Hindenberg and Ludendorff. . . . It stands among the renowned associations of Great Captains in history.

The World Crisis.

Mr. Churchill epitomised the association by inventing for it a joint monogram —thus—⊢L. He clearly had in mind the association of Marlborough and Eugene.

During the whole war the Germans never lost in any phase of the fighting more than the French whom they fought and frequently inflicted double casualties upon them. . . . In all the British offensives, the British casualties were never less then three to two and often nearly double the corresponding German losses.

The World Crisis.

Mr. Churchill completely disproved the claims made for a 'war of attrition' by giving the relative casualties. It is, however, not irrelevant that the Germans could stand their lesser casualties less than the Allies could stand greater.

From the moment when he received the news of the total evacuation of the Gallipoli Peninsula, the opportunity of General von Falkenhayn, Chief of the German

General Staff, was to pronounce the word 'Roumania'. He pronounced instead the word 'Verdun'.

The World Crisis.

This is not the only passage in which Mr. Churchill disputes the infallibility of the German General Staff. Falkenhayn, in his memoirs, however, gives the reasons which induced him to attack Verdun. He hoped to bleed the French Army to death. So he did, in fact, but the army did not die until twenty-five years later.

The total defeat of Germany was due to three cardinal mistakes: the decision to march through Belgium, regardless of bringing Britain into the war; the decision to begin the unrestricted U-boat war, regardless of bringing the United States into the war; and thirdly, the decision to use the forces liberated from Russia in 1918 for a final onslaught in France.

The World Crisis.

The faithful armies were beaten at the front and demoralised from the rear. The proud, efficient Navy mutinied. Revolution exploded in the most disciplined and docile of States. The Supreme War Lord fled.

The World Crisis. On the German collapse in 1918.

In the sphere of force, human records contain no manifestation like the eruption of the German volcano. For four years Germany fought and defied the five continents of the world by land, sea, and air. . . . Surely, Germans, for history it is enough! Is this the end? Is it merely to be a chapter in a cruel and senseless story? . . . Will our children bleed and gasp again in devastated lands? Or will there spring from the very fires of conflict that reconciliation of the three giant combatants which would unite their genius and secure to each in safety and freedom a share in rebuilding the glory of Europe?

The World Crisis.

Upon the brow from which the diadem of empire had been smitten he [Mr. Lloyd George] would have set a crown of martyrdom; and Death, with an all-effacing gesture, would have re-founded the dynasty of the Hohenzollern upon a victim's tomb.

Great Contemporaries.

On the ex-Kaiser. One of the slogans at the General Election of 1918 was 'Hang the Kaiser'. It fortunately proved impossible to induce the Dutch to give up the posturing refugee, and he was allowed to stagnate in growing oblivion and obscurity.

The draft treaty presented to the Germans prescribed the absolute cession of Upper Silesia, after the Ruhr the richest iron and coal district in the German Empire, to the Poles. This was the greatest blot upon the draft treaty with Germany. . . .

The moulds into which Central and Southern Europe has been cast were hastily and in part roughly shaped, but they conformed for all practical purposes with much exactness to the general design; and according to the lights of the twentieth century that design seems true.

The World Crisis.

The great objective of the Prime Minister's [Mr. Lloyd George's] policy has been . . . to be their [the Bolsheviks'] protectors and sponsors before Europe. I have been unable to discern any British interest, however slight, in this.

Letter to Lord Curzon, April 26, 1922.

The Treaty of Locarno may be regarded as the Old World counterpart of the Treaty of Washington. . . . These two august instruments give assurance to civilisation. They are the twin pyramids of peace rising solid and unshakable on either side of the Atlantic.

The World Crisis. Internal evidence suggests that this passage was written about 1928.

Hindenburg had nothing to learn from modern science and civilisation except its weapons; no rule of life but duty. . . . In the last phase we see the aged President, having betrayed all the Germans who had re-elected him to power, joining reluctant and indeed contemptuous hands with the Nazi leader. There is a defence for all this . . . he had become senile.

Great Contemporaries.

When Hitler began, Germany lay prostrate at the feet of the Allies. He may yet see the day when what is left of Europe will be prostrate at the feet of Germany.

Great Contemporaries.

There can never be friendship between the British democracy and the Nazi power—that power which spurns Christian ethics, which cheers its dupes onward by a barbarous paganism, which vaunts the spirit of aggression and conquest, which derives strength and perverted pleasure from persecution, and uses, as we have seen, with pitiless brutality the threat of murderous force.

Speech on the Munich Agreement, October 5, 1938.

Is he [Hitler] going to try to blow up the world or not? The world is a very heavy thing to blow up! An extraordinary man at a pinnacle of power may create a great explosion, and yet the civilised world may remain unshaken. The enormous fragments and splinters of the explosion may clatter down upon his own head and destroy him . . . but the world will go on.

Speech at the City Carlton Club, June 28, 1939.

Thus by every device, from the stick to the carrot, the emaciated Austrian donkey is made to pull the Nazi barrow up an ever-steepening hill.

Letter, July 6, 1938. Mr. Churchill is referring to the consequences of Hitler's rape of Austria in 1938.

Two years ago it was safe [to stand up to the dictators], three years ago it was easy, and four years ago a mere dispatch might have rectified the position. But where shall we be a year hence? Where shall we be in 1940?

Speech in the House of Commons, March 24, 1938.

Mr. Lansbury said just now that he and the Socialist Party would never consent to the rearming of Germany. But is he quite sure that the Germans will come and ask him for his consent before they rearm? Does he not think they might omit that formality and go ahead without even taking a card vote of the T.U.C.?

Speech in the House of Commons, November 7, 1933.

Sir John Simon said it was the first time Herr Hitler had been made to retract in any degree. [The course of events] can be very simply epitomised. . . . £1 was demanded at the pistol's point [at Berchtesgaden]. When it was given, £2 were demanded at the pistol's point [at Godesberg]. Finally [at Munich] the dictator consented to take £1 17s. 6d. and the rest in promises of goodwill for the future.

We have sustained a total and unmitigated defeat.

The German Dictator, instead of snatching the victuals from the table, has been content to have them served to him, course by course.

Silent, mournful, abandoned, broken, Czechoslovakia receded into the darkness. . . . I think you will find that in a period of time which . . . may be measured only by months, she will be engulfed in the Nazi regime.

Speech in the House of Commons on the Munich Agreement, October 5, 1938.

The proud German Army by its sudden collapse, sudden crumbling and breaking up, has once again proved the truth of the saying 'The Hun is always either at your throat or your feet'.

Speech to U.S. Congress, May 19, 1943.

I repeat the prayer around the louis d'or: 'Dieu protége la France.'

Broadcast to France, October 21, 1940.

The legend in question ran round the rim of the French twenty-franc Roya gold piece, where English coins are milled. The same legend is also found on coins of Napoleon as First Consul, both the five-franc and the twenty-franc coins.

For good or for ill the French people have been effective masters in their own house, and have built as they chose upon the ruins of the old regime. They have done what they like. Their difficulty is to like what they have done.

Letter, September 18, 1936.

Frenchmen! For more than thirty years in peace and war I have marched with you, and I am marching still along the same road.
Broadcast to France, October 21, 1940.

All my life I have been grateful for the contribution France has made to the glory and culture of Europe—above all for the sense of personal liberty and the rights of man that has radiated from the soul of France.
Speech in the House of Commons, August 2, 1944.

By all kinds of sly and savage means he [Hitler] is plotting and working to quench for ever the fountain of characteristic French culture and of French inspiration to the world. . . . Never will I believe that the soul of France is dead.
Broadcast to France, October 21, 1940.

The reasons why France does not present herself in her full strength at the present time are not to be found among the working masses, who are also the soldiers of France, but in certain strata of the middle-class and the well-to-do. Something of this kind can also be seen in Great Britain.
Letter, December 1, 1938.

France, though armed to the teeth, is pacifist to the core.
Speech in the House of Commons, November 23, 1932.

There was at this time in Britain a tendency to believe that France was needlessly militarist and obstructing disarmament. Hitler's flying start in the following year was not a little due to this obsession.

Anglo-French relations were at their worst. . . . But, after all, these had been only superficial difficulties, like bad manners between good friends.
The World Crisis.

We can see more clearly across the mists of time how Hannibal conquered at Cannae than why Joffre won at the Marne.

The World Crisis.

Fortune lighted his [Foch's] crest. . . . In 1914 he had saved the day by refusing to recognise defeat. In 1915 and 1916 he broke his teeth upon the Impossible. But 1918 was created for him.

Great Contemporaries.

This is at once too flattering and too censorious. In 1914 Foch nearly lost the war by his conduct of the battle of Morhange. In the two subsequent years his attacks in Picardy and on the Somme were relatively successful. The verdict on 1918 is correct.

Pétain was of all others fitted to the healing task . . . he thus restored by the end of the year [1917] that sorely tried, glorious army upon whose sacrifices the liberties of Europe had through three fearful campaigns mainly depended.

The World Crisis.

General (afterwards Marshal) Pétain had to deal with the mutineers in the French Army after the failure of Nivelle's offensive in 1917. Though he was known as the 'victor of Verdun', his success in quelling this mutiny is by far his truest title to fame.

In the last four years I have had many differences with General de Gaulle, but I have never forgotten, and can never forget, that he stood forth as the first eminent Frenchman to face the common foe in what seemed to be the hour of ruin of his country, and possibly of ours.

Speech in the House, August 2, 1944.

I have never lost my faith in the French Army— never!

Speech in Paris after liberation, November 12, 1944.

I hold no brief for Admiral Darlan. Like myself, he is the object of the animosities of Herr Hitler and of Monsieur Laval. Otherwise I have nothing in common with him.

We all thought General Giraud was the man for the job and that his arrival would be electrical. In this opinion, General Giraud emphatically agreed.

Speech in the House of Commons in secret session, December 10, 1942. On the Anglo-American landings in North Africa on November 8.

Darlan, the Vichy second-in-command, who was on a visit to Algiers, threw in his lot with the Allies. His services were accepted and used by General Eisenhower. The condonation of his former co-operation with the enemy was hotly criticised. As part of the invasion, General Giraud had been helped by submarine to escape from France. He fought bravely in 1940, had escaped from the Germans into then 'unoccupied' France early in 1942, and it was thought that he would dissuade the French in Algeria from resisting our landing.

I declare to you . . . even now, when misguided or subnormal Frenchmen are firing upon their rescuers . . . my faith that France will rise again.

Speech at the Mansion House, November 10, 1942. At that moment French resistance to the Allied landings in North Africa had not ceased.

Skeletons with gleaming eyes and poisoned javelins glare at each other across the ashes and rubble heaps of what was once the august Roman Empire.

Europe, the Mother Continent and fountain source not only of the woes, but of most of the glories of modern civilisation.

From an article in Collier's on the need for a United States o Europe, December 1946.

I am now going to say something that will astonish you. The first step in the re-creation of the European family must be a partnership between France and Germany. In this way only can France recover the moral

and cultural leadership of Europe. There can be no
revival of Europe without a spiritually great France
and a spiritually great Germany.

Speech at Zurich, September 19, 1946.

It may be that the father, or son, or a friend . . . is
called out and taken off into the dark, and no one knows
whether he will ever come back again, or what his fate
has been. There are millions of humble homes in
Europe . . . where this fear is the main pre-occupa-
tion of family life. . . .

Elections have been proposed in some of these Bal-
kan countries where only one set of candidates is
allowed to appear and where . . . the governing party
. . . is the only one which has the slightest chance.
Chance, did I say? It is a certainty.

Speech in the House, August 16, 1945.

Mr. Churchill was referring to conditions behind the 'iron curtain' in Soviet-
controlled Europe.

Even an isolationist would, I think, go so far as to
say: 'If we have to mix ourselves up with the Continent,
let us, at any rate, get the maximum of safety from our
commitments.'

Speech in the House, March 24, 1938.

Mr. Churchill was arguing for a defensive alliance with France as a deterrent
to Hitler. There was, at the time, an idea that we should not again have to send
an army to the Continent, but could limit ourselves to naval and air action and to
munition-making.

Quite apart from the good sense and moderation
for which the Japanese Government have become renowned . . .

Speech on the Navy Estimates, March 17, 1914. *Mr. Churchill
was endorsing the renewal of the Anglo-Japanese Alliance.*

Japan, with all her treachery and greed, remains un-subdued. The injury she has inflicted . . . and her detestable cruelties call for justice and retribution.

Broadcast, May 8, 1945.

Mr. Churchill was recalling that, even though Germany had capitulated, another enemy remained. He was particularly insistent because the Americans, to whom Japan was the nearest and longest enemy of the two, had agreed to contribute so much to the defeat of Germany before the defeat of Japan.

Should Germany at any time make war in Europe, we may be sure that Japan will immediately light a second conflagration in the Far East.

From a letter, November 27, 1936.

China, as the years pass, is being eaten by Japan like an artichoke, leaf by leaf.

Letter, September 3, 1937.

I must admit that, having voted for the Japanese alliance nearly forty years ago and having always done my very best to promote good relations with the Island Empire of Japan; and always having been a senti-mental well-wisher to the Japanese and an admirer of their many gifts and qualities, I should view [war with them] with keen sorrow.

Speech at the Mansion House, November 10, 1941, just a month before Pearl Harbour.

These [secret] societies [in Japan], dazzled and dizzy with their own schemes of aggression and the prospect of early victories, have forced their country against its better judgment into war.

Speech to the American Congress, December 26, 1941.

The Japanese, whose game is what I may call to make hell while the sun shines . . .

Speech in the House, January 27, 1942.

To-night the Japanese are triumphant. They shout their exultation round the world. We suffer. We are taken aback. We are hard pressed. But I am sure even in this dark hour that 'criminal madness' will be the verdict which history will pronounce upon the authors of Japanese aggression.

Broadcast, February 15, 1942, after the fall of Singapore.

If we are together nothing is impossible, and if we are divided all will fail.

Speech at Harvard on Anglo-American co-operation, August 1943.

They [the United States in July 1918] also proposed to send a detachment of the Young Men's Christian Association to offer moral guidance to the Russian people.

The World Crisis.

In spite of his American affinities, Mr. Churchill has never hesitated to criticise the substitution of gestures for policy.

On the one hand, one hundred million strong, stood the young American democracy. On the other cowered furtively, but at the same time obstinately, and even truculently, the old European diplomacy. Here young, healthy, hearty, ardent millions, advancing so hopefully to reform mankind. There, shrinking from the lime-lights, cameras and cinemas, huddled the crafty, cunning, intriguing, high-collared, gold-laced diplomatists. Tableau! Curtain! Slow music! Sobs; and afterwards chocolates!

The World Crisis.

This is another instance of Mr. Churchill's exasperation with the jejune ideas about Europe entertained in some quarters in America, and notably by President Wilson.

Should the United States become involved in war with Japan, the British declaration will follow within the hour.

Speech at the Mansion House, November 10, 1941, made—in vain —to deter the Japanese from entering the war.

It would have been better for us to have said to the United States: 'Build whatever you will; your Navy is absolutely ruled out of our calculations, except as a potential friend.'

Speech in the House, May 13, 1932.

Mr. Churchill was attacking the Treaty of London, embodying a measure of naval disarmament, on the ground that it forbade us to meet our special naval problems.

There are few virtues which the Poles do not possess and there are few errors they have ever avoided.

Speech in the House, after the Potsdam Conference.

An embarrassing situation arose after victory in 1945 out of Russian claims on former Polish territory and the predominance of Russian influences in Warsaw. Mr. Churchill was torn between recognition of the outstanding Polish valour in the Allied cause and the complete intransigence of some of the exiled Poles.

The soul of Poland is indestructible . . . she will rise again like a rock, which may for a spell be submerged by a tidal wave, but which remains a rock.

Speech in the House, October 1, 1939.

But it must be vividly impressed upon the Government of Poland that the accession of Soviet Russia in good earnest to the peace bloc of nations may be decisive in preventing war, and will in any case be necessary for ultimate success. One understands readily the Polish policy of balancing between the German and the Russian neighbour, but from the moment when the Nazi malignity is plain, a definite association between Poland and Russia becomes indispensable.

Letter, May 4, 1939.

Every week his [Hitler's] firing-parties are busy in a dozen lands. Monday he shoots Dutchmen; Tuesday, Norwegians; Wednesday, French or Belgians stand against the wall; Thursday it is the Czechs who must suffer; and now there are the Serbs and the Greeks to fill his repulsive bill of executions. But always, all the days, there are the Poles.

Message to the Polish people, May 3, 1941.

I have no hostility for the Arabs. I think I made [as Colonial Secretary] most of the settlements over fourteen years ago governing the Palestine situation. The Emir Abdullah is in Transjordania, where I put him one Sunday afternoon in Jerusalem. But I cannot conceive that you will be able to reconcile the development of the policy of the Balfour Declaration with an Arab majority on the Legislative Council.

Speech in the House, September 24, 1936.

Mr. Churchill has always been an upholder of the Balfour Declaration, which promised a National Home in Palestine to the Jews.

The Arab was an African reproduction of the Englishman; the Englishman a superior and civilised development of the Arab.

The River War.

To compare the life and lot of the African aboriginal —secure in the abyss of contented degradation, rich in that he lacks everything and wants nothing—with the long nightmare of worry and privation, of dirt, and gloom, and squalor, lit only by gleams of torturing knowledge and tantalising hope, which constitutes the lives of so many poor people in England and Scotland, is to feel the ground tremble underfoot.

My African Journey.

A palace intrigue secured the throne to Prince Thee-baw, and the new reign was inaugurated by an indiscriminate massacre of the king's other sons, with their mothers, wives, and children. Eight cartloads of butchered princes of the blood were cast, according to custom, into the river. The less honourable sepulchre of a capacious pit within the gaol was accorded to their dependants.

Lord Randolph Churchill.

On conditions in Burma before the British annexation, carried out when Lord Randolph was Secretary of State for India.

All the vigorous nations of the earth have sought and are seeking to conquer. Even the feeblest cling to their possessions with desperation. The Spaniards fought for the last remains of their Empire with the last remains of their strength. Few features strike the reader of modern Egyptian history so strongly as the desire of educated classes to hold or regain the Sudan. In a nation where public spirit is almost unknown, Cherif Pasha resigned rather than consent to the abandonment of the southern provinces. Even cataleptic China protests against dismemberment.

The River War.

As soldiers, they lack both vices and virtues.

The River War. On the Egyptian cavalry.

Whatever is set to the Mahdi's account, it should not be forgotten that he put life and soul into the hearts of his countrymen and freed his native land from foreigners.

The River War.

On this principle of giving the devil his due, Mr. Churchill sometimes said much the same about Hitler in the latter's early days; but he never mistook the devil for an angel.

I do not reproach the Dutch, our valiant allies of bygone centuries, dwelling as they do in the cage with the tiger, but when we are asked to take as a matter of course interpretations of neutrality which . . . inflict all the disadvantages upon the defenders of freedom, I recall a saying of the late Lord Balfour: 'This is a singularly ill-contrived world, but not so ill-contrived as that.'

Broadcast, March 30, 1940.

Mr. Churchill was addressing all the neutrals in an attempt to show that neutrality was impossible.

The recognition of their language is precious to a small people.

Speech in the House, July 31, 1906, on the Transvaal Constitution.

If the Chinese now suffer the cruel malice and oppression of their enemies, it is the fault of the base and perverted conception of pacifism their rulers have ingrained for two or three thousand years in their people.

Letter, September 3, 1937.

Venizelos is entitled to plead that in going to Smyrna he acted as mandatory for the four greatest Powers, but he went as readily as a duck will swim.

The World Crisis.

The reference is to the Greek expedition to Ionia in 1920. It was en ouraged, particularly by Mr. Lloyd George, who had inherited Gladstone's antipathy to the Turks. Two years later it led to the rout of the Greek Army by Mustapha Kemal and the complete collapse of the Peace Treaty with Turkey and of all M. Venizelos's lifelong dreams of a Greater Greece.

Whether Greece is a monarchy or a republic is a

matter for Greeks and Greeks alone to decide. All we
wish you is good, and good for all.

Speech in Athens, December 26, 1944.

After the liberation of Greece an attempt was made by the Left-wing organisation known as E.L.A.S. to seize power. The British forces checked the attempt.
Mr. Churchill paid a visit to Athens to see what was happening, principally
because he had been accused of suppressing democracy in Greece.

Where clusters of petty parties have each their own
set of appetites, misdeeds, or revenges . . .

*Speech in the House, January 1945. On the difficulty of forming
and keeping a Coalition in Greece.*

A boa constrictor, who had already covered his prey
with his foul saliva and then had it suddenly wrested
from his coils, would be in an amicable mood compared with Hitler . . . and the rest of the Nazi gang
when they experienced this bitter disappointment.

Speech in the House, April 9, 1941.

On March 27 a revolution took place in Yugoslavia which overthrew the pro-
Axis Government. Unhappily, that Government had so disposed the Yugoslav
Army that it proved impossible to concentrate forces in time to make any sort
of a fight against the German invasion.

'Love of Ireland' are the words which Sir John
Lavery has inscribed on his picture of the dead Irish
leader. They are deserved; but with them there might
at the end be written also 'To England Honour and
Good Will'. A great Act of Faith had been performed
on both sides of the Channel, and by that Act we dearly
hoped that the curse of the centuries would at last be
laid.

Thoughts and Adventures. On Michael Collins.

This great act of faith on the part of the stronger
Power will not, I believe, be brought to mockery by
the Irish people. If it were, the strength of the Empire

will survive the disappointment, but the Irish name
will not soon recover from the disgrace.

Speech on the Irish Treaty, May 31, 1922.

Mr. Churchill had taken a leading part in the negotiations with the Sinn Fein
leaders which led to the setting up of the Irish Free State.

Let us now see what is the interest of Southern Ireland in this matter. What is their heart's desire more
than anything else? (*Hon. Members:* A Republic.) Not
at all; that is a delusion, and my hon. Friends are
absolutely at sea when they say so. A Republic is an
idea most foreign to the Irish mind, associated with the
butcheries of Cromwell in their minds and foreign to
all the native genius of the Irish race, which is essentially monarchical.

(*Major C. Lowther:* Why have they an Irish Republi-
can Army if it is so foreign to them?)

Irish Free State Bill—Second Reading, February 16, 1922.

There is a deal of substance in Mr. de Valera's
declaration that the Irish would resent the landing of
any foreign Power upon their shores. . . . But it seems
to me that the danger is . . . that Ireland might be
neutral.

Speech in the House, May 5, 1938.

Mr. Churchill was protesting against the Chamberlain Government's agreement to hand over to Eire the ports reserved for British naval use under the Irish
Treaty of 1920.

The Spaniards have long memories; and I was not
surprised when, in the Great War, they showed themselves extremely frigid towards a combination which
included the descendants of the Napoleonic invaders,
the United States who had stripped them of the last

vestiges of their Colonial Empire, and Great Britain
. . . who still held Gibraltar.

Great Contemporaries.

The Spaniards, to whom democratic institutions
carry with them the hope of some great new advance
and amelioration, regarded Alfonso [XIII] as an
obstacle to their progress. The British and French
democracies . . . regarded the king as a sportsman;
the Spaniards knew him as a ruler.

Great Contemporaries.

Some people think that our foreign policy towards
Spain is best expressed by drawing comical or even
rude caricatures of General Franco; but I think there
is more in it than that.

Speech in the House, May 24, 1944.

Malta is the first instance of an air force being main-
tained against odds often of ten to one from a few air-
fields, all under constant bombardment. . . . It may
be that presently the German air forces attacking Malta
will have to move eastward to sustain the impending
offensive against Southern Russia. If so, we shall have
topped the ridge.

Speech in the House in secret session, April 23, 1942.

We shall continue to operate on the Italian donkey
at both ends—with a carrot and with a stick.

*Reply at Press Conference in America, May 1943, when asked how
a wobbling Italy would be treated.*

CHAPTER IX

ON POLITICS

Broad, simple, liberal safeguards and conceptions which are the breath of our nostrils in this country and which sustain the rights and freedoms of the individual against all forms of tyranny, no matter what liveries they wear or what slogans they mouth . . .

Speech in the House, September 28, 1944.

No one is compelled to serve great causes unless he feels fit for it, but nothing is more certain than that you cannot take the lead in great causes as a half-timer.

Speech at Chingford, May 8, 1936, on the Government's half-hearted sanctions policy during the Italo-Abyssinian War.

Marlborough was a Tory by origin, sentiment, and profession. But he was quite cool about whether the Government was Tory or Whig. What he sought was a political system that would support the war. He shared none of Anne's strong feelings about the High Church or Low Church bishops. Unity at home, and in Parliament to sustain, with the combined resources of the nation, the war abroad against the power of France was his sole and only end.

Marlborough.

We cannot say 'the past is the past' without surrendering the future.

Speech in the House, March 14, 1938.

I said that if I could have foreseen the General Strike and the coal stoppage I should not have felt justified in making a remission in taxation.

Mr. Pethick Lawrence: I do not deny that. The right hon. Gentleman, like a bad bridge player, blames his cards.

Mr. Churchill: I blame the crooked deal.

Budget Proposals, April 15, 1930.

Hatred plays the same part in government as acid in chemistry.

The World Crisis.

They saw that if he resigned he would put himself in the wrong. To dismiss him was dangerous: to provoke his resignation comparatively safe. Then they could have filled England with the cry that he had deserted his post on party grounds, that he had cast away the cause of the Allies, that he had ruined the peace which otherwise was in their hands. Any disaster in the field which followed his withdrawal they could lay on him. In fact, their conduct towards him during their first months exceeded in malice and in meanness anything which is known—and it is a wide field—in the relations of a British General with a British Government.

Marlborough.

When good people get into trouble because they are attacked and heavily smitten by the vile and wicked, they must be very careful not to get at loggerheads with one another.

Broadcast to France, October 21, 1940.

Mr. Churchill was appealing to the French not to listen to the Vichy anti-British propaganda.

I suppose we are admirers of the party system of government; but I do not think that we should any of us carry our admiration of that system so far as to say that the nation is unfit to enjoy the privilege of managing its own affairs unless it can find someone to quarrel with and plenty of things to quarrel about.

Speech in the House, December 17, 1906.

I am not going to follow the right hon. Member for Ross and Cromarty in the arguments he has used as to whether the money raised by the Motor Licence Duties was for all time finally assigned to the upkeep of the roads. I went through all that last year. At that time the argument used was that it belonged to the motorists and that it was 'government of the motorists, by the motorists, for the motorists'. . . . I am not fighting that battle this year. I fought it last year. I am merely pursuing, and collecting some of the baggage which they left behind.

Debate on the Budget, April 4, 1927.

This is a Government of the duds, by the duds, for the duds.

Remark on the present Government attributed to Mr. Churchill, but possibly apocryphal.

I accept their tributes, belated though they be, for what they are worth. I suppose a favourable verdict is always to be valued, even if it comes from an unjust judge or a nobbled umpire.

Speech in the House, April 20, 1931.

The occasion was Mr. Snowden's Budget, in which Mr. Churchill professed to find endorsement of the principles which he himself had followed as Chancellor of the Exchequer.

Chivalrous gallantry is not among the peculiar characteristics of excited democracy.

Savrola.

In six months' time it will not be the Socialist Government that will be in the dock; but the Government of the day; and those whom I shall never cease to declare have very largely brought these misfortunes upon us will once again be the airy and irresponsible critics of the administration, will once again be boasting of all they could do if only they came back into power.

Debate on Financial Situation, September 8, 1931.

Whatever one may think about democratic government, it is just as well to have practical experience of its rough and slatternly foundations.

Great Contemporaries.

Every new administration, not excluding ourselves, arrives in power with bright and benevolent ideas of using public money to do good. The more frequent the changes of Government, the more numerous are the bright ideas; and the more frequent the elections, the more benevolent they become.

Financial Statement, April 11, 1927—the post-General Strike Budget.

The long battle that I have waged over this 6d. off the Income Tax is over. For four years I successfully defended that remission. I defended it against the assaults of the General Strike—I beg pardon, the assaults of the difficult events of 1926. But at last I am beaten. Mr. Snowden and his party have had their way. . . . The popularity of the measure is assured by reducing the number of taxpayers involved to limits where the voting powers of those who are left may be considered negligible.

Speech in the House, April 15, 1930.

Marlborough, viewing the situation with military eye, had no intention of being brought to battle on ground which was so suited to the enemy. He and Godolphin therefore presented an oblique front to Rochester's formidable advance. They avoided his thrust by a practice, which even in our own reformed days is not unknown, of affirming their support for the principle of a Bill while taking steps to get it killed behind the scenes.

Marlborough.

I was not invited to the conference that took place last week in Downing Street between the Prime Minister and the leader of the Liberal party, but 'my hon. friend the Member for Treorchy' gave me a very shrewd account of the interview between the two party leaders. After the usual compliments, the Prime Minister said: 'We have never been colleagues, we have never been friends—at least, not what you would call holiday friends—but we have both been Prime Minister, and dog don't eat dog. Just look at this monstrous Bill the trade unions and our wild fellows have foisted on me. Do me a service, and I will never forget it. Take it upstairs and cut its dirty throat.'

Speech on the Trade Disputes and Trade Unions (Amendment) Bill, January 28, 1931.

The 'Member for Treorchy' was the *nom de plume* of a political journalist.

Politicians rise by toil and struggles. They expect to fall; they hope to rise again.

Great Contemporaries.

There is scarcely anything more important in the government of men than the exact—I will even say the pedantic—observance of the regular forms by which the guilt or innocence of accused persons is determined.

My African Journey.

I do not think we are likely to learn much from the liquor legislation of the United States.

Budget speech, April 11, 1927.

Civilisation must be armed with machinery if she is to subdue these wild regions [tropical Africa] to her authority. Iron roads, not jogging porters; tireless engines, not weary men; cheap power, not cheap labour; steam and skill, not sweat and fumbling—there lies the only way to tame the jungle—more jungles than one.

My African Journey.

What about mining royalties? In all this talk about the importance of cheap coal to our industries and to the poor consumer we have had no mention of mining royalties. No. We never mention that.

Speech on the Hours Bill, July 6, 1908.

Mining royalties were bought out by the Coalition Government during the war of 1939-45.

I am the oldest living champion of Insurance in the House of Commons. . . . In 1909 I obtained the power to spread a network of [labour] exchanges over the whole of Great Britain and Ireland. For that purpose we [the then Liberal Government] brought into the public service—Mr. Beveridge.

Broadcast, June 13, 1945.

The so-called 'Beveridge plan' for comprehensive social insurances had created a furore when published during the war. Part of the Socialist case at the election of 1945 was that the Churchill Government did not genuinely mean to implement it. Mr. Churchill was here replying to this charge and pointing out that it was he who gave Sir William (now Lord) Beveridge his first chance.

Labour exchanges are the gateway to industrial security.

Speech in the House, February 17, 1909.

The two systems [labour exchanges and unemployment insurance] are complementary; they are man and wife; they mutually support and sustain each other.

Speech in the House, May 19, 1909.

It is in the interests of trade unionists, who are long-established contributors, as well as the employers in industries, to make sure that there is not growing up a certain habit of learning how to qualify for the unemployment insurance.

Speech in the House, September 29, 1925.

If I had my way I would write the word 'insure' over the door of every cottage, and upon the blotting-book of every public man, because I am convinced that by sacrifices which are inconceivably small, which are all within the power of the very poorest man in regular work, families can be secured against catastrophes which otherwise would smash them up for ever.

On National Insurance: speech in Manchester, May 23, 1909.

There is a real opportunity for bringing the magic of averages to the rescue of millions.

Broadcast, 1942, on a four-year plan for post-war reconstruction.
The allusion is to the ratio between insurance contributions and benefit.

And if a rise in stocks and shares confers profits on the fortunate holders far beyond what they expected, or, indeed, deserved, nevertheless that profit has not been reaped by withholding from the community the land which it needs, but, on the contrary, apart from mere gambling, it has been reaped by supplying industry with the capital without which it could not be carried on.

Why land should be taxed and not stocks and shares. Speech in Edinburgh, July 17, 1909.

Mr. Churchill was in full cry for the Lloyd George Budget, which included duties on increment values in land. The event was to show that they were a total failure.

To dispute the authority of a newly elected Parliament is something very like an incitement to violence on the part of the other House.

This was a speech made at the beginning of the controversy between the Liberal Government and the House of Lords, which resulted in the Parliament Act, limiting the power of the Lords to reject Bills passed by the Commons.

Lord Lansdowne has explained, to the amusement of the nation, that he claimed no right on behalf of the House of Lords to 'mince' the Budget. All, he tells us, he has asked for, so far as he is concerned, is the right to 'wince' when swallowing it. Well, that is a much more modest claim. It is for the Conservative party to judge whether it is a very heroic claim for one of their leaders to make. If they are satisfied with the wincing Marquis, we have no reason to protest.

Speech on the Budget at Norwich, July 16, 1909.

I proceed to inquire on what principle the House of Lords deals with Liberal measures. The right hon. Member for Dover by an imaginative effort assures us that they occupy the position of the umpire. Are they even a sieve, a strainer, to stop legislation if it should reveal an undue or undesirable degree of Radicalism or Socialism?

Speech on the House of Lords, June 29, 1907.

It is just about 100 years since the publication of *Sybil* [by Disraeli], a work of fiction that was not only a literary but also a political event. Few novels have made a deeper or more lasting impression upon the political thought of a nation.

Message to the Primrose League, December 31, 1944.

He seems to think that all Governments must be infallible and all rebels must be vile. It all depends on what is Government and what are rebels.

Speech in the House, April 14, 1937.

I acted with great promptitude. In the nick of time, just as Mr. Snowden was rising with overwhelming fury, I got up [and withdrew the tax on kerosene]. Was I humiliated? Was I accused of running away? No! Everyone said: 'How clever! How quick! How right!' Pardon me referring to it. It was one of my best days.

Speech in the House, June 1937.

The question at issue was the National Defence Contribution proposed by Neville Chamberlain. Mr. Churchill was asking for its withdrawal and quoting from his own experience when Chancellor of the Exchequer to show that *amour propre* should not frustrate the dropping of an unpopular tax.

There are two ways in which a gigantic debt may be spread over new decades and future generations. There is the right and healthy way; and there is the wrong and morbid way. The wrong way is to fail to make the utmost provision for ammortisation which prudence allows, to aggravate the burden of the debt by fresh borrowing, to live from hand to mouth and from year to year, and to exclaim with Louis XVI: 'After me, the deluge!'

Budget Speech, April 11, 1927.

Of this Budget speech [April 1927] Mr. Snowden observed: 'The right hon. Gentleman was faced by difficulties which would have been the despair of most men. The right hon. Gentleman is not like most men. Those who expected that he would come here this afternoon in a proper mood of penitence and humility, and appropriately dressed in sackcloth, did not know the right hon. Gentleman. He is not that sort. Excuses he may make, but apologies never. He lives in a realm of imagination. He glories in big figures. If he cannot have a big surplus, then he must have a big deficit. He is like Charles VII of France, of whom it was said: "No man ever lost a kingdom with more gaiety".'

It cannot, in the opinion of His Majesty's Government, be classified as slavery in the extreme acceptance of the word without some risk of terminological inexactitude.

Speech in the House, February 22, 1906.

The Liberal Party had been elected at the General Election of this year by an enormous majority. One of the issues had been their allegation that 'Chinese slaves' were being imported to labour in the Rand mines. This is what would be called to-day an over-simplification of the question—the persons in question being indentured labourers. Mr. Churchill's way of admitting electionitis became famous.

At any time or in any place, here on the floor of the House of Commons or in the tumult of a popular election, we are ready to meet you on the issue and . . . prove to the country that you are wrong all along the line—wrong in your logic, wrong in your statecraft, wrong in your arithmetic, wrong even in your demagogy—right only in having at last the candour and courage to avow your true opinions and, by so doing, warn the public throughout the Empire of the catastrophe from which they have been preserved.

Speech in the House, February 20, 1907.

This challenge was to the Conservative party on the question of Tariff Reform

The right hon. Member for Carnarvon Boroughs [Mr. Lloyd George] is going to borrow £200,000,000 and to spend it . . . upon paying the unemployed to make racing tracks for well-to-do motorists to make the ordinary pedestrian skip; and we are assured that the mere prospect of this has entirely revivified the Liberal party. At any rate, it has brought one notable recruit. Lord Rothermere, chief author of the anti-waste campaign, has enlisted under the Happy Warrior of Squandermania.

Budget speech, April 15, 1929.

The detailed method of spending the money has not yet been fully thought out, but we are assured on the highest authority that if only enough resource and energy is used there will be no difficulty in getting rid of the stuff. This is the policy which used to be stigmatised by the late Mr. Thomas Gibson Bowles as the policy of buying a biscuit early in the morning and walking about all day looking for a dog to give it to. At any rate, after this, no one will ever accuse the right hon. Gentleman of cheap electioneering.

Budget speech, April 15, 1929.

Mr. Lloyd George had produced elaborate proposals for 'conquering unemployment', mainly through large-scale public works. Mr. Churchill was contending that most of them would be useless and wasteful.

I remember many years ago Mr. Lloyd George sending for me to receive with him a deputation of hop-growers. . . . We could give them nothing but sympathy, but we gave them a double dose of that.

Speech on introducing the Budget, April 28, 1925.

Mr. Churchill could afford the confession, because he was imposing a 'nakedly protective' duty on hops.

We are often told that the gold standard will shackle us to the United States. I will deal with that in a moment. I will tell you what it will shackle us to. It will shackle us to reality. For good or for ill, it will shackle us to reality.

Speech on the Gold Standard Bill, April 4, 1925.

Take the case of the backer. . . . Does anyone suppose that a man or woman who now bets with a credit bookmaker, who has only to go to the telephone and make his wager by word of mouth under the full sanction of the law, who has every facility of the public service at his disposal, who can make his wager with a firm in which he has the uttermost confidence—can you suppose that this backer is going, for the sake of avoiding a deduction from his winnings of the odds equal to one shilling in the pound or to avoid a deduction from his winnings of one shilling in the pound, to wander around a particular district in some manufacturing town looking for a mysterious individual into whose hand he may surreptitiously place half a dollar.

Speech in the House, April 28, 1926.

Mr. Churchill, as Chancellor of the Exchequer, was defending his proposa to tax betting, which had been attacked on the ground that bookmakers and backers had only to transact their business in the street in order to evade the tax. In spite of this defence, the tax was a failure.

I remember it was the fashion in the Army when a court-martial was being held and the prisoner was brought in that he should be asked if he objected to being tried by the President or to any of those officers who composed the court-martial. On one occasion a prisoner was so insubordinate as to answer: 'I object to the whole —— lot of you.' That is clearly illustrative of the kind of reception which, at this stage, consultation of the trade unions by the Government would meet with.

Speech in the House, February 9, 1927.

We shall not allow any prejudice against individual personalities engaged in this conflict to complicate our task. But you cannot ask us to take sides against arithmetic.

Speech on the Coal Dispute, August 31, 1926.

Mr. Churchill had taken a prominent part in the unsuccessful attempt to settle this dispute after the collapse of the General Strike. He is referring to the stormy personality of A. J. Cook, the miners' leader; and to the fact that there was a world glut of coal which, failing arrangements such as a subsidy, prevented high wages in the mining industry.

But when the right hon. Gentleman tells us that we are going to take away the workers' only bargaining power I must ask him one or two questions. Is a general strike—which, whether intentionally or not, is inevitably against the Constitution—a necessary part of the workers' bargaining power in trade methods? (*An hon. Member:* Certainly!) I do not seem to get a very decided answer to that. Is mass intimidation at a works or at a man's home an essential part of the reasonable collective bargaining power of the trade unionists of the country? . . . Is collecting money for Socialist candidates from Liberal and Conservative trade unionists an essential part of the workers' collective bargaining power?

Speech in the House, February 9, 1927.

The references are to practices proposed to be banned by the Trade Disputes Bill, which was the legislative aftermath of the General Strike.

The Trade Union Congress have only to cancel the General Strike and withdraw the challenge they have issued and we shall immediately begin, with the utmost care and patience with them again, the long, laborious task which has been pursued over these many weeks of endeavouring to rebuild on economic foundations the prosperity of the coal trade. That is our position. No door is closed.

Debate on Industrial Crisis, May 3, 1926.

But I warn you—I warn you that if ever there is another General Strike we will let loose another *British Gazette.*

Speech in the House after the collapse of the General Strike, 1926.

During the strike the Government published a newspaper of its own, called the *British Gazette*, of which Mr. Churchill was in charge. It was an object of derision to professional journalists, and Mr. Churchill wisely turned its failings into a joke.

We now know with accuracy the injury which has been done, at any rate to our finances. We meet this afternoon under the shadow of last year. It is not the time to bewail the past; it is the time to pay the bill. It is not for me to apportion the blame; my task is only to apportion the burden. I cannot present myself before the Committee in the guise of an impartial judge; I am only the public executioner.

Financial Statement, April 11, 1927—the post-General Strike Budget.

His second maxim was as follows: 'Take office only when it suits you, but put the Government in a minority whenever you decently can.'

Lord Randolph Churchill.

There is no situation to which it cannot address itself with vigour and ingenuity. It is the citadel of British liberty. It is the foundation of our laws.

Speech on the House of Commons in the House of Commons, October 28, 1942.

The essence and foundation of House of Commons debating is formal conversation. The set speech, the harangues addressed to constituents, or to the wider public out of doors, has never succeeded much in our small, wisely built chamber.

Great Contemporaries.

The old House of Commons, destroyed in the blitz, held only about two-thirds of the elected members. It was, and its new edition will be, rectangular, in contrast to other legislative chambers, which are semi-circular. The advantages of opponents facing each other instead of being adjacent are very great.

It seems to me—and I have a lengthening experience in the House—that false arguments very rarely pay in debate: (*An hon. Member*) You are using them now. I always try to economise the use of false arguments as much as possible, because a false argument is so often detected, and it always repels any listener who is not already a convinced and enthusiastic partisan.

Speech in the House, April 28, 1926.

The right hon. Member for Colne Valley [Mr. Snowden] is not, I am sorry to say, in his place. He told me that he had a public engagement to take part in one of the impending by-elections. We may imagine him, in our thoughts, in a few minutes' time, addressing a far less critical assembly than this, and repeating to them the same stream of Parliamentary Billingsgate with which he favoured us last night.

Speech in the House, April 28, 1926.

Deep down in the heart of the old-fashioned Tory, however unreflecting, there lurks a wholesome respect for the ancient forms and safeguards of the English Constitution, and a recognition of the fact that some day they may be found of great consequence and use.

Lord Randolph Churchill.

It would be easy to give an epitome of the financial year which has closed. The road has lain continually uphill, the weather has been wet and cheerless, and the Lords Commissioners of His Majesty's Treasury have been increasingly uncheered by alcoholic stimulants. Death has been their frequent companion and almost their only friend.

Budget speech, April 24, 1928.

The reference is to the fact that in the previous year only the death duties had yielded according to expectations.

I look forward to the universal establishment of minimum standards of life and labour, and their progressive elevation as the increasing energies of production may permit. I do not think that Liberalism in any circumstances can cut itself off from this fertile field of social effort, and I would recommend you not to be scared in discussing any of these proposals, just because some old woman comes along and tells you they are Socialistic.

Speech at Glasgow, October 11, 1906.

They will be invited to continue in office on sufferance in order that if they are violent they may be defeated, and if they are moderate they may be divided.

Letter on the formation of a minority Socialist Government in 1924.

Socialism is inseparably interwoven with totalitarianism and the abject worship of the State. Look how even to-day they [the Socialists] hunger for controls of every kind as if these were delectable foods instead of wartime inflictions. . . . This State is to be the arch-employer, the arch-planner, the arch-administrator and ruler, and the arch-caucus-boss.

Broadcast, June 4, 1945.

No Socialist system can be established without a political police. . . . They would have to fall back on some form of Gestapo—no doubt very humanely directed in the first instance.

Broadcast, June 4, 1945.

This is the statement which, some critics thought, lost the election of 1945. The public did not recognise even the *umbra* of a Gestapo in Socialist personalities and policy.

Between us and the orthodox Socialists there is a great doctrinal gulf, which yawns and gapes. . . . There is no such gulf between the Conservative and National Government I have formed and the Liberals. There is scarcely a Liberal sentiment which animated the great Liberal leaders of the past which we do not inherit and defend.

Broadcast, June 4, 1945.

During the election campaign which followed victory over Germany some of the Liberal party insisted on running candidates of their own. Mr. Churchill felt their defection keenly. He has always been a natural Coalitionist, and on this occasion had not expected the Liberal leaders to leave him.

If I had proposed to take £12,000,000 from the Navy, all the Liberal party would have been bound to rise up and say: 'Hosanna! Let us, if you will, have a second- or third-class Navy, but, whatever happens, we must have first-class roads.'

Debate on the Budget, April 4, 1927.

Is this Coalition to be above party government or below party government?

Speech in the House on the formation of a National Government in 1931.

It is no use leading other nations up the garden and then running away when the dog growls.

Speech in the House, June 1937. Mr. Churchill was speaking in support of non-intervention in Spain.

On the one hand, the cries of a drowning man; on the other, good advice from one who had no intention of going into the water.

The World Crisis.

The particular reference is to the British failure (and inability) to support the Greek venture into Asia Minor when it looked like coming (and came) to disaster in 1921-22.

The war [of 1914-18] had been fought to make sure that the smallest State should have the power to assert its lawful rights against even the greatest; and this will probably be for several generations an enduring fact.

The World Crisis. Even Homer nods!

When I first went into Parliament, now nearly forty years ago . . . the most insulting charge which could be made against a Minister . . . short of actual malfeasance, was that he had endangered the safety of the country . . . for electioneering considerations.' Yet such are the surprising qualities of Mr. Baldwin that what all had been taught to shun has now been elevated into a canon of political virtue.

Letter, December 11, 1936.

Mr. Baldwin had explained that if he had told the people 'Germany is rearming and we must rearm', his party would most likely have lost the General Election of 1935, in the then pacifist mood of the nation.

In those days Mr. Baldwin was wiser than he is now; he used frequently to take my advice.

Speech in the House, May 22, 1935.

Mr. Churchill is recalling the Conservative vote against the Treaty of London.

Some people say: 'Put your trust in the League of Nations.' Others say: 'Put your trust in British rearmament.' I say we want both. I put my trust in both.

Speech in the House, October 24, 1935.

What is the point in crying out for the moon when you have the sun, when you have the bright orb of day in whose refulgent beams all the lesser luminaries hide their radiance?

Speech in the House, February 1938.

The reference is to the appointment of Lord Halifax—a peer—as Foreign Secretary in the place of Mr. Eden. Mr. Churchill was arguing that there was no need for a Foreign Secretary in the Commons, since the Prime Minister was there. The quotation is part of a sustained piece of sarcasm. The point is that the Prime Minister was insisting upon being virtually his own Foreign Secretary in pursuit of a policy of appeasement. Another gem from the same speech was the reference to Mr. Ernest Brown, then Minister of Labour. Mr. Churchill examined his claims to be Foreign Secretary and exclaimed that 'never since Cromwell would such a voice have gone out'. Mr. Brown is the possessor of a particularly resonant voice.

In dealing with nationalities, nothing is more fatal than a dodge. Wrongs will be forgiven, sufferings and losses will be forgiven or forgotten, battles will be remembered only as they recall the martial virtues of the combatants; but anything like chicane, anything like a trick, will always rankle.

Speech in the House on the conciliation of South Africa, April 5, 1906.

I am anxious above all things, that we should arrive at a perfectly clear understanding of what is the official policy of. the Labour party in regard to the Balfour Note and the debt settlements. We have a right to know it. The country has a right to know, the House a right to know, and the world has a right to know what is the view which the official Opposition takes of the contractual and responsible and plighted obligations of the State.

Budget debate, April 17, 1929.

Mr. Snowden had threatened to repudiate the Balfour Note on war debts, which declared that we should ask no more from our debtors than we had to pay to our creditors.

We cannot have our relations with our nearest neighbour destroyed and impaired by the prejudice and ill-feeling, personal ill-feeling, of a single individual, however eminent he may be, nor has anyone a right to twist or distort the foreign policy of a party or of a country merely because in the course of his political activities he has been led into taking up an utterly untenable and indefensible position.

Budget debate, April 17, 1929.

They [the Chamberlain Government] neither prevented Germany from rearming, nor did they rearm ourselves in time. They quarrelled with Italy without saving Ethiopia. They exploited and discredited the vast institution of the League of Nations. They neglected to make alliances and combinations which might have repaired previous errors; and thus they left us in the hour of trial without adequate national defence or effective international security.

Speech on the Munich Agreement, House of Commons, October 5, 1938.

A day would come when powerful nations, beginning to recover from the war, and to gather their power together again, would become the cause of rumours in this country. There would be rumours that in the heart of Germany or Russia there were great aerial developments of a very serious character, or of a character which might easily have a military complexion. Then you would have a war scare, and I have no doubt you would have a leading article in *The Times* on that subject. (*Interruptions.*)

Speech in the House, March 1, 1920.

My friend, Mr. Boothby, in his speech jeered at the expression 'collective security'. What is there ridiculous about collective security? The only thing that is ridiculous about it is that we have not got it.

Speech in the House, March 14, 1938, in the debate on Hitler's seizure of Austria.

Mr. Churchill has always been against 'splendid isolation'. The constructive side of his anti-appeasement campaign was a call for effective organisation of the League of Nations. He has always realised that a small nation in a crowded island on Europe's doorstep cannot save itself without (*a*) allies, (*b*) military efficiency of its own. Hence his consistent devotion to the Empire, to Anglo-American understanding, to the League, and most recently to the concept of the United States of Europe.

By this time next year we shall know whether the policy of appeasement has appeased, or whether it has only stimulated a more ferocious appetite.

Letter, November 17, 1938. We actually knew within ten months.

I stand by my original programme—blood, toil, tears, and sweat . . . to which I added five months later 'many shortcomings, mistakes, and disappointments'.

Speech in the House, January 27, 1942.

I have never made any predictions, except things like saying Singapore would hold out. What a fool and a knave I should have been to say it would fall!

Speech in the House on the motion censuring the 'central direction of the war', July 2, 1942.

This was the only session during the war upon which the House of Commons attempted to censure the Government. It had been gravely alarmed by Rommel's victory in Libya, which drove the Eighth Army back to Alamein; and on the very day of the debate there were strong rumours that the Alamein position had been pierced.

It is because things have gone badly and worse is to come that I demand a Vote of Confidence.

Speech in the House, January 27, 1942.

I have read this document to the House because I am anxious that Members should realise that our affairs are not conducted entirely by simpletons and dunderheads.

Speech in the House in secret session, April 23, 1942.

The document was an Admiralty prediction that the two German battleships at Brest would try to sail home through the Channel. They did—successfully— and Mr. Churchill was answering criticism that they had fooled us.

I am sure that the mistakes of that time will not be repeated; we shall probably make another set of mistakes.

Speech in the House, June 8, 1944, on being asked to avoid the mistakes made after the war of 1914-18.

When this new Parliament first met all the Socialist Members stood up and sang the 'Red Flag' in their triumph. Peering ahead through the mists and mysteries of the future . . . I see the division at the next election will be between those who wholeheartedly sing the 'Red Flag' and those who rejoice to sing 'Land of Hope and Glory'.

Speech at Blackpool, October 5, 1946.

Let us look at food. The German U-boats in their worst endeavour never made bread rationing necessary in war. It took a Socialist Government and Socialist planners to fasten it on us in time of peace when the seas are open and the harvests good.

Speech to the Conservative Conference, Blackpool, October 5, 1946.

If you strike at savings you at once propagate the idea of 'Let us eat, drink and be merry, for to-morrow we die'. That is at once the inspiration and the mortal disease by which the Socialist philosophy is affected.

Speech in the House, May 19, 1927.

And now the British housewife, as she stands in the queues to buy her bread ration, will fumble in her pocket in vain for a silver sixpence. Under the Socialist Government nickel will have to be good enough for her. In future we shall still be able to say: 'Every cloud has a nickel lining.'

Speech at Blackpool, October 5, 1946.

The reference is to the Socialist Government's decision to substitute a cupro-nickel for a silver coinage.

The disease of defeat was Bolshevism. . . . The disease of victory was different. It was an incapacity to make peace.

From a letter, November 11 (Armistice Day), 1937.

The dark ages may return—the Stone Age may return on the gleaming wings of science; and what might now shower immeasurable material blessings upon mankind may even bring about its total destruction. Beware I say! Time may be short.

Speech at Fulton, Missouri, March 5, 1946.

The reference is to the discovery of how to release atomic energy.

It is a mistake to look too far ahead. Only one link in the chain of destiny can be handled at a time.

Speech in the House after the Yalta Conference, 1945.

Mr. Maurice Webb (to Mr. Churchill): We are rather like a lot of sheep, aren't we? *Mr. Churchill:* Yes, bloody black sheep.

Note.—*This story is told by Mr. Webb in his speech in the House of Commons, October 29, 1946.*

They want to reduce us to one vast Wormwood Scrubbery.

Speech in the House, March 12, 1947.

The reference is to the alleged determination of the Labour Government to control our daily lives through bureaucrats, just as the prison authorities control the inmates of Wormwood Scrubs through gaolers.

We must build a kind of United States of Europe.

Speech at Zurich, September 19, 1946.

CHAPTER X

MAXIMS ON HUMAN CONDUCT

It is a fine thing to be honest, but it is also very important to be right.

Remark upon Mr. Baldwin, whose honesty was proverbial.

It is better to be frightened now than killed hereafter.

Speech in the House, February 1934. The context was a warning that the Germans already had a military air force.

Never to surrender ourselves to servitude and shame, whatever the cost and the agony may be.

Broadcast, May 19, 1940.

We shall draw from the heart of suffering itself the means of inspiration and survival.

Broadcast, September 11, 1940.

There is no less likely way of winning a war than to adhere pedantically to the maxim of 'safety first'.

Speech in the House, April 10, 1941.

There is only one answer to defeat, and that is victory.

Speech in the House, June 10, 1941.

I see them guarding their homes, where mothers and wives pray—ah, yes, for there are times when all pray—for the safety of their loved ones. . . .

Broadcast, June 22, 1941.

When Hitler invaded Russia. 'Them' are the Russian soldiers. The point is that Russia was then officially atheistical.

However tempting it might be to some, when much trouble lies ahead, to step aside adroitly and put someone else up to take the blows, I do not intend to take that cowardly course, but, on the contrary, to stand to my post and persevere in accordance with my duty as I see it.

Speech in the House, February 25, 1942.

This speech was made at the peak of disaster in the Far East. Mr. Churchill was explaining that he could not devolve more upon other Ministers, in answer to the criticism that he was trying to do too much himself.

Men may make mistakes, and learn from their mistakes. . . . Men may have bad luck, and their luck may change.

Speech in the House, July 2, 1942, in reply to Vote of Censure.

You must never make a promise [to an ally] which you do not fulfil.

Speech in the House, November 11, 1942.

Mr. Churchill was explaining that he had never promised Russia to open a second front in Europe in that year.

We cannot have a band of drones in our midst, whether they come from the ancient aristocracy, the modern plutocracy, or the ordinary type of pub-crawler.

Broadcast on the Four-Year Plan, 1943.

There is a precipice on either side of you—a precipice of caution and a precipice of over-daring.

Speech in the House, September 21, 1943.

Don't argue the matter. The difficulties will argue for themselves.

Memo to the Chief of Combined Operations, May 30, 1942.

The subject is piers for use on beaches, which afterwards developed into the artificial harbour used at Arromanches in the Normandy landings.

There is all the difference in the world between a man who knocks you down and a man who leaves you alone.

Speech in the House, May 24, 1944.

Mr. Churchill was demurring to attacks on General Franco, and observing that he had at least remained neutral.

We must beware of needless innovations, especially when guided by logic.

Reply in the House, December 17, 1942, when asked to rename the Minister of Defence and the Secretary of State for War, on the ground that their titles were illogical.

The butterfly is the Fact—gleaming, fluttering, settling for an instant with wings fully spread to the sun, then vanishing in the shades of the forest. Whether you believe in Free Will or Predestination, all depends on the slanting glimpses you had of the colour of his wings.

My Early Life.

Don't give your son money. As far as you can afford it, give him horses.

Advice to parents from My Early Life.

Trying to paint a picture is like trying to fight a battle. It is, if anything, more exciting than fighting it successfully. But the principle is the same. It is the same kind of problem as unfolding a long, sustained, interlocked argument.

Thoughts and Adventures. Mr. Churchill likes to amuse himself and interest others by painting in oils.

Learn to get used to it. Eels get used to skinning.

Notes for a speech delivered in secret session, June 20, 1940. 'It' was being bombed.

Surely we must have an opinion between Right and Wrong? Surely we must have an opinion between Aggressor and Victim?

Speech in Manchester, May 9, 1933.

Mr. Churchill was disclaiming that his attack on appeasement was due to any preconceived political ideology.

Courage is rightly esteemed the first of human qualities, because . . . it is the quality which guarantees all others.

Great Contemporaries.

It is hard, if not impossible, to snub a beautiful woman—they [*sic*] remain beautiful and the rebuke recoils.

Savrola.

Three times is a lot.

The World Crisis.

Mr. Churchill is explaining how three chances of securing an 'annihilating victory' at the Battle of Jutland had been missed.

The fortunes of mankind in its tremendous journeys are principally decided for good or ill—but mainly for good, for the path is upward—by its greatest men and its greatest episodes.

Tribute to Lord Halifax, January 9, 1941.

To-day we may say aloud before an awestruck world: 'We are still masters of our fate. We are still captains of our souls.'

Speech in the House, September 9, 1941. The phrase is borrowed from Henley's 'Out of the night that covers me'.

When you have to hold a hot coffee-pot, it is better not to break the handle off until you are sure that you will get another equally convenient and serviceable, or, at any rate, until there is a dishcloth handy.

Speech in the House, February 22, 1941.

A medal glitters; but it also casts a shadow.

Speech in the House, March 22, 1944.

Mr. Churchill was arguing against too profuse an award of war decorations, and explaining that whatever definition of entitlement was devised, there would be some just disqualified who would feel heartburnings.

It is not open to the cool bystander, who afterwards becomes the loyal and ardent comrade and brave rescuer, to set himself up as an impartial judge of events which would never have occurred had he out-stretched a helping hand in time.

The World Crisis. The reference is to America's neutrality from 1914 to 1917.

If truth is many-sided, mendacity is many-tongued.

History cannot proceed by silences. The chronicler of ill-recorded times has none the less to tell his tale. If facts are lacking, rumour must serve. Failing affidavits, he must build with gossip.

Marlborough.

Everybody who knew Townshend loved him. This last must always be considered a dubious qualification.

Marlborough.

Noble spirits yield themselves willingly to the successively falling shades which carry them to a better world or to oblivion.

Marlborough.

Comfortable feather heads in their feather beds in New York, Paris, and London might give a passing thought to the tremendous drama and tragedy [of China].

Letter, November 3, 1938.

All Imperialism is not 'claptrap'. We ought to distinguish between the amateur Imperialists who gave their lives in the field and the professional Imperialists who got their living by practising it in politics.

Speech in the House, May 16, 1904.

This truth is incontrovertible. Panic may resent it; ignorance may deride it; malice may distort it; but there it is.

Speech in the House, May 17, 1915. The reference is to the proved superiority of the aeroplane over the airship.

Physician, comb thyself.

Speech in the House, May 23, 1916. Retort to the War Office, which was asking for the 'combing-out' of industries and other Departments.

Consideration for the lives of others and the laws of humanity, even when one is struggling for one's life and in the greatest stress, does not go wholly unrewarded.

Speech in the House, February 2, 1917.

Parliament can compel people to obey or to submit, but it cannot compel them to agree.

Speech in the House, September 27, 1926.

A hopeful disposition is not the sole qualification to be a prophet.

Speech in the House, April 30, 1927.

In the art of drafting [Income Tax Law] there seems to be a complete disdain of the full stop, and even the humble colon is an object to be avoided.

Speech in the House, April 19, 1927.

There is no real gain to British democracy when some family leaves the home of its ancestors and hands it over to a transatlantic millionaire or wartime profiteer.

Speech in the House, April 15, 1930, *against too high rates of surtax and death duties.*

We have all heard of how Dr. Guillotine was executed by the instrument he invented . . .

(*Sir H. Samuel:* He was not.)

Well, he ought to have been.

Speech in the House, April 29, 1931.

I used to be much affected by a popular drama called *The Girl Who Took the Wrong Turning.*

Speech in the House, June 26, 1931.

Miss Bondfield was Minister of Labour in the Labour Government of 1929-31. Mr. Churchill is referring to her downfall in consequence of being unable to check the rising tide of unemployment.

In sport, in courage, and in the sight of Heaven, all men meet on equal terms.

The Malakand Field Force.

Nature will not be admired by proxy.

The Malakand Field Force.

Mr. Churchill is explaining why he refrains from expatiating on the loveliness of a moon-lit valley on the North-West Frontier.

A bullet in the leg will make a brave man a coward. A blow on the head will make a wise man a fool. Indeed, I have read that a sufficiency of absinthe can make a good man a knave. The triumph of mind over matter does not seem to be quite complete as yet.

The Malakand Field Force.

It may seem strange to speak of polo as an imperial factor, but it would not be the first time in history that national games have played a part in high politics.

The Malakand Field Force.

Mr. Churchill is speaking of the contribution of polo to good relations between Indians and British.

Soberness and restraint do not necessarily prevent the joyous expression of the human heart.

Retort to Mr. Aneurin Bevan, May 1, 1945.

Mr. Bevan had urged that the fact that a large number of troops were still engaged in the Far East would exercise a 'sobering restraint' on jubilation over the victory in Europe.

This revelation of the secrets of nature, long mercifully withheld from man, should arouse the most solemn reflections in the mind and conscience of every human being capable of comprehension. We must indeed pray that these awful agencies will be made to conduce to peace among the nations, and that instead of wreaking measureless havoc upon the entire globe they may become a perennial fountain of world prosperity.

Statement on the atom bomb, August 6, 1945.

Since they were henceforth to be doomed to an enforced and inviolable chastity, the cause of their satisfaction is as obscure as its manifestation was unnatural.

The River War.

The reference is to the Mahdi's wives, who were asserted by Slatin Pasha to be secretly delighted at the death of their husband.

Nothing daunted the valiant heart of man. Son of the Stone Age, vanquisher of nature with all her trials and monsters, he met the awful and self-inflicted agony with new reserves of fortitude. . . . The vials of wrath were full: but so were the reservoirs of power.

The World Crisis.

Down the ages, above all other calls, comes the cry that the joint heirs of Latin and Christian civilisation must not be ranged against one another.

Appeal to Mussolini to remain neutral in 1940, *to which 'a dusty answer' was returned. The reader will detect the same note as in Mr. Churchill's recent appeals for a United States of Europe.*

Five or ten years' experience as a Member of this House [of Commons] is as fine an all-round education in public affairs as any man can obtain.

Speech in the House, February 27, 1941.

No idea is so outlandish that it should not be considered with a searching but at the same time with a steady eye

Speech in the House, May 23, 1940.

The essential structure of the ordinary British sentence . . . is a noble thing.

My Early Life.

I had no idea in those days of the enormous and unquestionably helpful part that humbug plays in the social life of great peoples.

My Early Life.

This reflection was provoked by a settlement of the controversy about the promenade of the old Empire Theatre in Leicester Square, which was attacked in the 'nineties as a haunt of vice. A compromise was reached whereby the bars were screened off from the promenade, so that they were not technically part of it. At the time, Mr. Churchill explains, he disdained this hypocritical settlement, but later was not so sure that in such matters humbug had not its uses.

Elderly people and those in authority cannot always be relied upon to take enlightened and comprehending views of what they call the indiscretions of youth.

My Early Life.

Although always prepared for martyrdom, I preferred that it should be postponed.

My Early Life.

As long as you are generous and true, and also fierce, you cannot hurt the world or even seriously distress her. She was made to be wooed and won by youth. She has lived and thrived only by repeated subjugations.

Always remember, however sure you are that you can easily win, there would not be a war if the other man did not think he also had a chance.

My Early Life.

Each day exactly like the one before, with the barren ashes of wasted life behind, and all the long years of bondage stretching out ahead.

My Early Life.

Mr. Churchill, having been a prisoner of war, is giving a picture of the feelings of an ordinary long-term prisoner, and explaining why, when Home Secretary, he tried to ameliorate prison life.

When by extraordinary chance one has gained some great advantage or prize and actually had it in one's possession and been enjoying it for several days, the idea of losing it becomes almost insupportable.

My Early Life.

Luckily, life is not so easy as all that; otherwise we should get to the end too quickly.

My Early Life.

Unpunctuality is a vile habit.
My Early Life.

It is better that one notability should be turned away expostulating from the doorstep than that nine just deputations should each fume for ten minutes in a stuffy ante-room.
My Early Life.
The theme is that if you are running late on a series of appointments it is better to cut out some altogether, so as to be in time for the rest.

All wisdom is not new wisdom.
Speech in the House, October 5, 1938.

Time is a changeable ally.
Broadcast, March 30, 1940.

I can never doubt which is the right end of the [telegraph] wire to be at. It is better to be making the news than taking it.
Remark prompted by his success at becoming a correspondent with the Malakand Field Force.

I cannot expect to be impartial between the fire-brigade and the fire.
Retort to charges that the British Gazette, of which he was Editor during the General Strike of 1926, was not impartial.

Things do not get better by being left alone. Unless they are adjusted, they explode with a shattering detonation.
The World Crisis.

The end comes often early to such men whose spirits are so wrought that they know rest only in action, contentment only in danger, and in confusion find their only peace.
Savrola.

They are decided only to be undecided, resolved to be irresolute, adamant for drift, all-powerful for impotence.

Remark on the Government of 1936.

Science burrows its insulted head in the filth of slaughterous inventions.

Article in the Evening Standard, September 1936.

Life is a whole, and luck is a whole, and no part of them can be separated from the rest.

Remark prompted by his survival of the charge of the Lancers at Omdurman, whereas the officer commanding the troops which he had expected to be leading was killed.